THE UNOFFICIAL

formula one legends: drivers, teams and cars

formula one legends:
drivers, teams and cars

that changed the course of history

mark hughes

southwater

Contents

This edition is published by Southwater

Southwater is an imprint of Anness Publishing Ltd
Hermes House, 88–89 Blackfriars Road, London SE1 8HA
tel. 020 7401 2077; fax 020 7633 9499
www.southwaterbooks.com; info@anness.com

© Anness Publishing Ltd 2004

UK agent: The Manning Partnership Ltd, 6 The Old Dairy, Melcombe Road
Bath BA2 3LR; tel. 01225 478444; fax 01225 478440
sales@manning-partnership.co.uk

UK distributor: Grantham Book Services Ltd, Isaac Newton Way
Alma Park Industrial Estate, Grantham, Lincs NG31 9SD
tel. 01476 541080; fax 01476 541061; orders@gbs.tbs-ltd.co.uk

North American agent/distributor: National Book Network, 4501 Forbes Boulevard
Suite 200, Lanham, MD 20706; tel. 301 459 3366; fax 301 429 5746
www.nbnbooks.com

Australian agent/distributor: Pan Macmillan Australia, Level 18, St Martins Tower
31 Market St, Sydney, NSW 2000; tel. 1300 135 113; fax 1300 135 103
customer.service@macmillan.com.au

New Zealand agent/distributor: David Bateman Ltd, 30 Tarndale Grove, Off Bush Road
Albany, Auckland; tel. (09) 415 7664; fax (09) 415 8892

A CIP catalogue record for this book is available from the British Library.

Publisher: Joanna Lorenz
Editor: Elizabeth Woodland
Production Controller: Darren Price
Senior Editor: Sarah Ainley
Text Editor: David Malsher
Design: Michael Morey
Photography: Sutton Motorsport Images

Previously published as part of a larger volume, *The Unofficial Complete
Encyclopedia of Formula One*

1 3 5 7 9 10 8 6 4 2

Introduction

It was man's very nature that made motor racing so inevitable. Clever enough to have devised the car, he is intrinsically competitive enough to have then made racing cars a mere formality. The ultimate form of the discipline came to be called Grand Prix racing in 1906, just 11 years into the sport's history, and Formula One Grands Prix are still the pinnacle of the sport today. What also remains, unaltered through over a century, is the essence of the sport. The qualities it demands of drivers, who face the ultimate stakes, and technicians, who experience the most intense of challenges, make it arguably the most majestic of all sporting endeavours.

▼ Jack Brabham, winner of the French Grand Prix, Reims, in 1966.

▼ The Italian Ferrari fans were out in force at Monza for the Italian Grand Prix, September 2001.

Though latterly it has become more overtly commercial than in the past, that is simply a reflection of the world in which the sport exists, just as the cars have mirrored the level of technological sophistication of the modern industrial world. It shouldn't be forgotten that motorsport was conceived as much with business in mind – by a group of pioneer car manufacturers – as it was for sport. Formula One owes its existence to business, and always has, but the superficial trappings melt away to nothing in the intensity of battle, once the start flag has dropped or the lights have gone out. Between that moment and the chequered flag, the sport exists in its purest form.

▼ The Tyrolean mountains provide a scenic backdrop for the Austrian Grand Prix.

▼ Allan McNish in the Toyota TF102 at the Monaco Grand Prix, Monte Carlo, 2002.

A–Z
Drivers

The same competitive urge to drive a machine faster than the next man has produced over a century of heroes. Through the ages of wildly differing machinery and circumstance, that basic urge has remained the same, as has the basic technique of balancing grip against power through steering and throttle control.

It was always a dangerous sport and despite the elimination of many unnecessary perils, it remains inherently so. Many of these heroes didn't get to live out the natural span of their lives. Here then are the men who excelled in a sport with the highest of stakes.

◄ The start of the Monaco
Grand Prix, Monte Carlo, 2002.

Jean Alesi

A spectacular Formula One career that lasted for over 12 years yielded only one victory but produced countless moments of high drama and astonishing car control.

Alesi graduated to Formula 3000 in 1988 as the French Formula Three Champion, and the following year he clinched the Formula 3000 crown with Eddie Jordan Racing. That season he made his Formula One debut with Tyrrell, making a big impression by coming home fourth in his first event. He created an even bigger impact in the first race of 1990, at Phoenix, when after leading in the Tyrrell and being passed by Ayrton Senna, he cheekily re-passed the great Brazilian before surrendering to the inevitable and finishing second.

Such performances led to a string of offers from top teams for 1991, among them Williams and Ferrari. In a decision of dubious wisdom, he chose the latter, then spent five years in a sequence of Ferraris that were rarely as quick as the top cars. His sole victory came in Canada in 1995, his final year with the Italian team.

Alesi spent the next six seasons in a succession of ever-less competitive cars from Benetton, Sauber and Prost. A mid-2001 switch to Jordan was a last gasp opportunity to regain form and rescue his career, but he was dropped at the end of the year.

Jean Alesi	
Nationality	French
Seasons	1989–2001
Teams driven for	Tyrrell, Ferrari, Benetton, Sauber, Prost, Jordan
Number of major victories	1

◄ Jean Alesi celebrates his first Grand Prix victory at Montreal, Canada, in 1995.

▼ (below) Alesi came second for Ferrari at the San Marino Grand Prix at Imola in 1995.

▼ (bottom) Jean Alesi, in the Ferrari 412T2, took second place at the German Grand Prix, Nürburgring, in 1995.

Fernando Alonso

By winning the 2003 Hungarian Grand Prix for Renault, Fernando Alonso became the youngest ever driver to win a Formula One race. It also marked the first time that a Spaniard had won a Grand Prix.

The 2003 season was Alonso's first with a competitive team, though he had made his debut with Minardi in 2001 as a 19-year-old. As a six-year-old he had been encouraged by his father – himself a keen amateur kart racer – to take up karting in Spain. Over the following years he became one of the country's top exponents of the sport, and this led to his graduation to car racing in 1999, when he won the Spain-based Formula Nissan Championship.

This gave him a test drive with Minardi and it led to a seat within the F3000 category, the stepping stone to Formula One. During this time Alonso's obvious talent was noticed by Renault Sport boss, Flavio Briatore, who put him on a long-term contract.

After his debut Formula One season with Minardi, he took up the position of test driver for the Renault team, and from there he graduated to a seat with the race team in 2003. His sensational form has led many to mark him out as the future successor to Michael Schumacher as the sport's number one driver, and has created an explosion of Formula One interest in Spain.

Fernando Alonso	
Nationality	Spanish
Seasons	2001–present
Teams driven for	Minardi, Renault
Number of major victories	1

◄ **Alonso has ignited Formula One interest in his native Spain.**

▼ **Alonso became the youngest-ever Grand Prix winner, at 22 years 26 days, when he triumphed in Hungary in 2003.**

▲ **Fernando Alonso's Renault has a comfortable lead at the 2003 Hungarian Grand Prix.**

Chris Amon

The brilliant New Zealander has the unfortunate reputation as the greatest driver never to win a Grand Prix. He began his Formula One career as a 19-year-old in 1963 – for many years he held the record as the youngest driver to start a Grand Prix – and ended it as a disillusioned 32-year-old in 1976. In between, he gave some virtuoso performances that stood comparison with any of the greats of the sport, but he added to his natural bad luck by a sequence of poor career moves.

Indulged by his farming father, Amon began racing in New Zealand, where he was spotted by Formula One team owner Reg Parnell, who took him into Formula One with his privateer team. Amon won the Le Mans 24 Hour sportscar race of 1966 in partnership with Bruce McLaren, but not until he signed with Ferrari for 1967 did his potential become clear. He took fourth in that year's championship, but in 1968, with a more competitive car, he was often the fastest man around. He retired from a 40-second lead in Spain and an even more dominant position in the closing stages in Canada. It seemed only a matter of time before such form gave him the world title.

▲ Chris Amon in 1968.

▼ Chris Amon's Ferrari 312 took second place at the British Grand Prix, Brands Hatch, in 1968.

Chris Amon	
Nationality	New Zealand
Seasons	1963–76
Teams driven for	Parnell, Cooper Ferrari, March, Matra, Tecno, Tyrrell, Amon, BRM, Ensign, Wolf
Number of major victories	0

In the non-championship Tasman series of 1967–68, he raced wheel-to-wheel with the great Jim Clark. In the same competition the following year, he triumphed over future champion, Jochen Rindt. He left Ferrari at the end of 1969, just as the team came good, and left March at the end of 1970, as it was on the verge of producing the car that would take Ronnie Peterson to second in the 1971 World Championship. In France in 1972, he drove one of the greatest races of all time when, after leading comfortably in his Matra, he suffered a puncture then came back to take third. After retiring in 1977 he returned home to New Zealand.

Mario Andretti

Often cited as the most versatile racing driver of all time, Andretti was a champion in Formula One and Indycar racing, and he has won in everything from dirt-track racing to NASCAR stock cars.

Of Italian descent, Andretti moved to America as a child. Together with his twin brother Aldo, he began racing dirt-track midget cars, leading eventually to a full-time drive in the USAC Championship that included the famous Indianapolis 500 race. As a rookie, he won the USAC Championship in 1965. At Indianapolis that year he came to the attention of Lotus boss Colin Chapman, who promised him a Formula One drive whenever he felt he was ready.

Mario Andretti	
Nationality	American
Seasons	1968–82
Teams driven for	Lotus, Ferrari, Parnelli, Alfa Romeo
Number of major victories	12

◀ **Mario Andretti won the 1978 World Championship driving for Lotus – taking six victories along the way.**

▼ **Mario Andretti took pole position and finished in third place as a Ferrari stand-in at the Italian Grand Prix, Monza, in 1982.**

He felt ready by the end of 1968 – and promptly put his Lotus on pole position on his Formula One debut at the American Grand Prix. He didn't race in Formula One full-time until 1976, but in between he won the 1971 South African Grand Prix for Ferrari. In 1976, he returned to Lotus, and together they won the final race of the year. This was a prelude to a brilliant two-season run with the ground-effect Lotus 78 and 79 models, culminating in the 1978 World Championship. Lotus' competitiveness went downhill subsequently, and Andretti spent his final Formula One season in 1981 with Alfa Romeo. Ferrari called him up as a stand-in at the 1982 Italian Grand Prix – and he responded with pole position, showing that at the age of 42, he still had it.

Thereafter, he finished off his career in American Indycar racing, winning for many years before finally retiring from motorsport at the end of 1994.

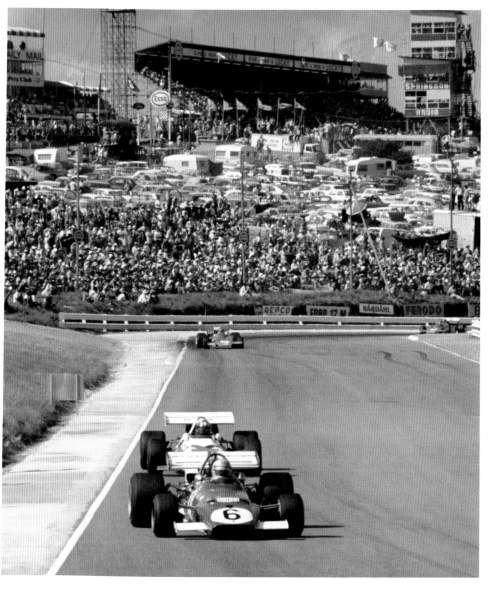

◀ **Winner Mario Andretti leads Jo Siffert at the South African Grand Prix, 1971.**

René Arnoux

Arnoux was one of the generation of French drivers of the 1970s who began their careers at the Winfield Racing Drivers' School and succeeded in each category as they moved up the ladder. Arnoux's progress wasn't as smooth as those of some of his peers, but when he got his big Formula One break in 1979, with Renault, he made maximum use of it. In a Formula One career lasting 11 years, he took 18 pole positions and seven race wins with Renault and Ferrari.

After winning the 1977 Formula Two Championship with the Martini team, they graduated to Formula One together in 1978. It was an underfunded effort and they struggled, but for 1979 Renault wanted to expand to running two of its radical turbocharged cars, and Arnoux's promise and nationality made him a shoe-in for the drive. He won his first Grand Prix in Brazil in 1980, and driving alongside Alain Prost in the

▼ *(below)* Winner René Arnoux in the Renault RE20 at the South African Grand Prix in 1980. It was his second victory.

following two years he proved every bit as fast, if not as calculating. After famously disobeying team orders to win the 1982 French Grand Prix, his days at Renault were numbered. For 1983 he was recruited by Ferrari.

He took three victories in his first season with the Italian team, entering the final round with an outside chance of taking the world title but ultimately finishing third. After performing erratically, he was sacked by Ferrari early in 1985 and this signalled the end of his frontline career. He returned with Ligier in 1986 and served out four more Formula One years before quietly retiring at the end of 1989.

◀ **René Arnoux was one of the fastest drivers of the early 1980s.**

▼ **(bottom) Arnoux, here in his final full season with Ferrari, at Austria in 1984. He won three times for the Italian team.**

René Arnoux

Nationality	French
Seasons	1978–89
Teams driven for	Martini, Renault, Ferrari, Ligier
Number of major victories	7

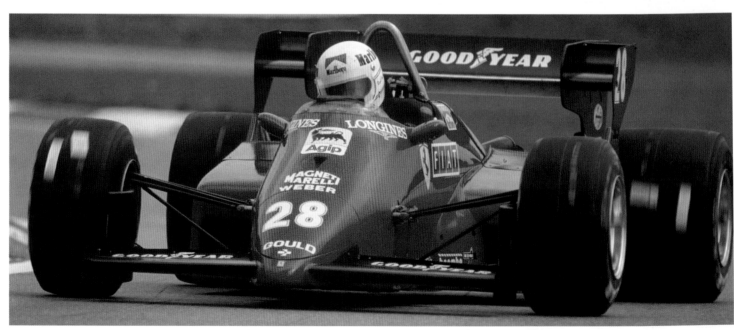

Alberto Ascari

The man who would be 1952 and 1953 World Champion was just seven years old when his father, Antonio, was killed while leading the 1925 French Grand Prix. Alberto subsequently began racing motorcycles and, just prior to the outbreak of World War II, he made his car racing debut.

Post-war, he was signed by Maserati and enjoyed considerable success there in 1948 and 1949. His senior team-mate Luigi Villoresi adopted him as his protégé and guided his subsequent career. In 1950, the pair were recruited by Ferrari, where they stayed for the next four years.

Ascari quickly demonstrated that he was the only driver on the same level as the legendary Juan Manuel Fangio, and the two had some epic dices. For 1952, the World Championship was changed from Formula One to Formula Two regulations, and Ferrari produced the fastest machine. It was under these circumstances that Ascari reeled off the most dominant championship display ever seen. He missed the first race to compete in the Indianapolis 500, but won every single subsequent round of the contest. Despite increased pressure from Fangio's Maserati in 1953, he took his second title quite comfortably. For 1954, he was recruited by Lancia but

Alberto Ascari	
Nationality	Italian
Seasons	1947–55
Teams driven for	Maserati, Ferrari, Alfa Romeo, Lancia
Number of major victories	15

◄ Alberto Ascari, driving a 2-litre Ferrari 500, celebrates his win at Silverstone, 1953.

▼ *(left)* Alberto Ascari and and Luigi Villoresi.

delays in readying the new D50 model meant he did very little racing. Highly superstitious, it has been claimed he was obsessed with the idea that destiny would not allow him to live longer than the 36 years his father had enjoyed.

At 36 years old, he was lying in second place in the 1955 Monaco Grand Prix when he crashed into the harbour. He was only slightly injured. A few days later, he visited Monza to watch his friend Eugenio Castellotti test a Ferrari sports car, before asking if he himself might try the car. In an accident that has never been fully explained, Ascari left the road and was killed.

▼ Alberto Ascari led the 1951 French Grand Prix in the Ferrari 375.

Antonio Ascari

Ascari worked his way into the racing seat through a succession of jobs as a mechanic and tester before World War I. Post-war, he established himself as an Alfa Romeo dealer in Milan, and through that connection began racing works Alfas.

This was at a time when the Milan-based company was just emerging as a serious Grand Prix force, and Ascari's arrival upon the international scene was sensational. In his first big-time event, Cremona 1924, he gave the brand new Alfa Romeo P2 a debut victory. He then came to within three laps of winning the French Grand Prix before going on to a dominant victory in Italy.

Within the space of a few months, Ascari had made serious claim to be the world's fastest Grand Prix driver. He opened his 1925 account with a start-to-finish victory in the Belgian Grand Prix. He was leading by a long way in the French Grand Prix of that year when rain began to fall, and everyone but Ascari reduced their pace considerably. But he pressed on, and eventually he slid wide. A rear wheel became entangled in some fencing, and the car flipped upside down. It was before the days of crash helmets or roll-over bars, and Ascari's injuries were fatal.

Antonio Ascari

Nationality	Italian
Seasons	1924–25
Teams driven for	Alfa Romeo
Number of major victories	2

▲ *(left)* Antonio Ascari for Alfa Romeo at Monza in 1924, his first year in Grand Prix.

▲ *(right)* Antonio Ascari *(left)* with young Alberto, seated in the car, and Enzo Ferrari *(second from left)*.

▼ Antonio Ascari driving for Alfa Romeo at the French Grand Prix, Montlhéry, 1925.

Rubens Barrichello

The other half to Michael Schumacher of the dominant Ferrari team, the Brazilian Rubens Barrichello has performed with distinction for four years alongside the champion. During that time he has won seven Grands Prix and he finished runner-up to Schumacher in the 2002 World Championship.

Prior to his stint at Ferrari, Barrichello had served a seven-year apprenticeship in Formula One with the Jordan and Stewart teams, showing regular flair and promise but never quite managing to win a race. After a successful karting career in Brazil, Barrichello came to Europe in 1990 and established a big reputation in the junior categories, winning the European GM Euroseries that year and following it up with victory in the 1991 British Formula Three Championship.

His Formula One debut came in 1993, with Jordan. In that year's European Grand Prix at Donington, he drove brilliantly to run in second position to his countryman and idol

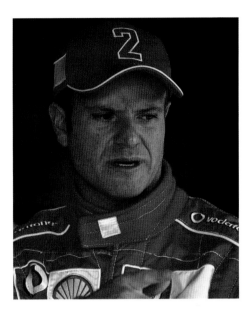

Ayrton Senna before retirement. It took a long time to convert such potential into Formula One success, but he finally achieved his first win at Hockenheim in the 2000 German Grand Prix.

He was at the centre of the Ferrari controversy in 2002 when the team instructed him to give way to his

Rubens Barrichello	
Nationality	Brazilian
Seasons	1993–present
Teams driven for	Jordan, Stewart, Ferrari
Number of major victories	7

◀ **Barichello has been a critical part of Ferrari's success into the new millennium.**

▼ **Barrichello takes victory in the 2003 Japanese Grand Prix.**

team-mate Schumacher in the Austrian Grand Prix, despite having led the race from the start. He complied in the last few hundred yards of the race, triggering an outcry from those who felt the team were doing the sport a disservice. In 2003, Barrichello won both the British and Japanese Grands Prix and was a critical element in securing Schumacher's record sixth title.

Robert Benoist

Benoist's Grand Prix immortality is assured by his feat of winning all four Grands Prix of 1927 for Delage.

The son of a Rothschild gamekeeper, he began racing bicycles and worked for the Grégoire car company shortly before World War I. He volunteered as a pilot for the war and survived being shot down; he was also credited with shooting down one enemy plane. After the war, he began cyclecar racing and was a dominant champion in 1923. This brought him to the attention of Delage, with whom he made his Grand Prix debut in 1924. He finished third in that year's European Grand Prix at Lyons. He then shared victory with team-mate Albert Divo in the 1925 French Grand Prix, after the Alfa team withdrew following the death of Antonio Ascari.

As the Delage became ever-more competitive, so Benoist's career flowered, culminating in his victorious 1927 season. Delage then withdrew from racing, leaving Benoist to serve the rest of his career with Bugatti, for whom he won the Le Mans 24 Hours sports car race in 1937.

Robert Benoist	
Nationality	French
Seasons	1924–36
Teams driven for	Delage, Bugatti
Number of major victories	5

During World War II Benoist was a leading member of the French resistance against German occupation, and he received training in Britain. Working in collaboration with fellow Grand Prix drivers William Grover-Williams and Jean-Pierre Wimille, he was highly successful in the field before being captured and executed by the Gestapo.

▲ Louis Chiron (left) and Benoist in 1928.

◀ Benoist in action at the European Grand Prix, San Sebastian, Spain, in 1926.

Gerhard Berger

In a Formula One career stretching from 1984 to 1997, Berger took victories with Benetton, Ferrari and McLaren, though he never managed a sustained challenge for the world title.

The Austrian's rise through the sport's junior ranks was rapid, and partly funded by his father's transport company. He made a big step from Renault Five racing to Formula Three in 1983, and was immediately competitive. By the end of 1984, he was making his Formula One debut in an ATS-BMW with over 800 horsepower. His abundant natural ability meant he adapted comfortably.

After a season driving for Arrows in 1985, he was recruited by the new Benetton team for 1986. At the end of that season he gave himself and the team their first victory, with a winning drive in Mexico. His performances had attracted the attention of Ferrari, with whom he scored two consecutive victories at the end of 1987.

In the early laps of the 1989 San Marino Grand Prix, a wing failure sent him into the wall at Imola's flat-out Tamburello corner. The impact was massive and the Ferrari erupted in flames. Remarkably, he was pulled out of the car with just slight burns to his hands, a broken rib and fractured shoulder blade. Two races later he was back behind the wheel.

▲ **Gerhard Berger in 1987, during the first of two stints driving for the Ferrari team. He won the final two races of that year.**

Gerhard Berger	
Nationality	Austrian
Seasons	1984–97
Teams driven for	ATS, Arrows, Benetton, Ferrari, McLaren
Number of major victories	10

In 1990, he was recruited by McLaren to partner Ayrton Senna, but he wasn't the same standard as the Brazilian. He served three years alongside Senna before returning to Ferrari for a big money offer. He helped improve the team's performances and won the 1994 German Grand Prix. He left in 1996, when Ferrari recruited Michael Schumacher, and returned to Benetton, where he served out his career, winning the 1997 German Grand Prix before retiring. He later took up the post of motorsport director with BMW.

▲ **Berger's Benetton locks a wheel on the way to third place in the 1997 Brazilian Grand Prix in Sao Paulo.**

▶ **Berger's Ferrari (left) attempts to fend off Damon Hill's Williams in the 1994 Canadian Grand Prix. Berger finished fourth, two places behind Hill.**

Georges Boillot

Boillot appeared like a meteor in Grand Prix racing, winning on his debut in France in 1912, and establishing himself as the fastest and most daring driver up to the outbreak of World War I. Serving as a pilot in the French Air Force, he was killed in action in 1916.

His car racing career began in the voiturette ("small car") class, with Lion-Peugeot, in 1908. He soon came to be the dominant driver of this category, and when Lion-Peugeot and the parent Peugeot company were reunited in 1911, he was central to the plan of building and racing a full-size Grand Prix car.

This car was the ground-breaking twin-cam, four-valve-per-cylinder L76. Boillot took it to victory on its debut at Dieppe. He repeated this result in the French Grand Prix of 1913, before setting pole position and a lap record

Georges Boillot

Nationality	French
Seasons	1912–14
Teams driven for	Peugeot
Number of major victories	2

▲ Georges Boillot finished first in the 1910 Mont Ventoux hill climb in the Lion-Peugeot.

▼ *(left)* Boillot won the Mont Ventoux hill climb in 1913 in the Peugeot 5.7 litre.

▼ *(right)* Georges Boillot.

on his debut at the Indianapolis 500 in 1914. Later that year, in the French Grand Prix, he drove a heroic race in a Peugeot that was, by now, outclassed by the latest model from Mercedes. He kept the faster German cars at bay for almost all of the race's seven-hour duration, but retired on the final lap with engine failure.

He was shot down after attempting to take on seven German scout planes single-handed. He was awarded a posthumous *Legion d'Honneur*.

Pietro Bordino

▼ Pietro Bordino driving for Fiat in the
2-litre Grand Prix of 1924.

As the lead driver with the crack
Fiat squad, Bordino was the man
to beat in the early 1920s.

He had begun as a Fiat riding
mechanic pre-war, alongside aces
Felice Nazzaro and Vincenzo Lancia. His
driving debut for Fiat was at the 1921
Brescia Grand Prix where his speed was
sensational, leading comfortably until
sidelined by mechanical problems.

Through 1922 and 1923, he won a
whole flurry of major Grands Prix, and
had there been a World Championship
then he would have won titles in both

years. Fiat withdrew from Grand Prix
racing at the end of 1924, and Bordino
wasn't seen for a while. The company
made a one-off comeback at the 1927
Milan Grand Prix, which Bordino
completely dominated.

He was practising for the 1928
Targa Florio race in a Bugatti when he
hit a dog, jamming his steering and
causing him to crash into a river with
fatal results.

◄ Bordino's new Fiat at the Monza
Grand Prix of 1927.

Pietro Bordino	
Nationality	Italian
Seasons	1921–28
Teams driven for	Fiat, Bugatti
Number of major victories	3

▼ Bordino – in the Fiat 802 – retired from
the 1921 Italian Grand Prix at Brescia but set
a lap record of 150.35km/h (93.43mph).

Jack Brabham

This tough Australian who began his career midget-racing on the cinder tracks of his home country won three World Championships, the last of them in a car bearing his own name. This stands as a unique achievement in the history of the sport.

After a highly successful career in Australia, Brabham arrived in Britain in 1955 and hooked up with the Cooper team. A highly technical driver, Brabham was able to help Cooper develop its mid-engined cars, first of all in sports cars and subsequently in Formula One.

In 1959, Brabham in the mid-engined Cooper emerged victorious from a final-round championship showdown against Tony Brooks in the front-engined Ferrari. It was the final nail in the coffin for the traditional Grand Prix car. Brabham repeated his success in 1960 but the Cooper was about to be leapfrogged by Lotus.

Sensing that Cooper was a spent force, Brabham set up on his own, recruiting his friend from midget-racing, Ron Tauranac, to design the

▲ Jack Brabham, in the Brabham BT33, taking his 14th and final Grand Prix victory at Kyalami, South Africa, in 1970.

Jack Brabham

Nationality	Australian
Seasons	1955–70
Teams driven for	Cooper, Brabham
Number of major victories	14

Brabham BT3, which made its debut in 1962. Brabham seemed content to let his employed driver Dan Gurney lead the team and was planning to retire from the wheel at the end of 1965. But then Gurney left to set up *his* own team, leaving Brabham as the lead driver once again. This coincided with the new 3-litre formula, and Brabham's shrewdness of engine choice and cockpit skills gave him his third title.

He remained a front rank driver until his retirement at the end of 1970, when, at the age of 44, he sold up and returned home to Australia.

▲ Brabham at the Mexico Grand Prix in 1969, where he finished the race in third place after starting from pole position.

◄ Brabham retired from the 1966 Italian Grand Prix at Monza, but he won that year's championship regardless.

Tony Brooks

Brooks vies with Stirling Moss as the greatest driver never to have won the World Championship, though his quiet, less thrusting manner meant he has never achieved the same fame as his contemporary.

Brooks came to prominence in 1955 when, in only his second race outside the British club scene, he won the Syracuse Grand Prix for Connaught. Although it was a non-championship event, this was the first Grand Prix victory for a British car and driver for over 30 years. On his aeroplane flights there and back, he was studying for his final exams in dentistry.

Although Brooks received the qualification, he never did take up dentistry, as his huge talent made him much in demand within the sport. After a season with BRM in 1956,

▲ Tony Brooks, driver for Vanwall, Aston Martin and Cooper cars, in 1958.

▲ Brooks winning the German Grand Prix at the Nürburgring for Vanwall in 1958.

Tony Brooks

Nationality	British
Seasons	1955–61
Teams driven for	Connaught, BRM, Vanwall, Ferrari
Number of major victories	6

he was recruited by Vanwall to drive alongside Moss in 1957. The pair proved extremely evenly-matched and took a shared victory in the British Grand Prix. Brooks won three times in 1958, helping Vanwall to the World Constructors' title.

For 1959, he moved to Ferrari and was unlucky to lose out in the title showdown with Jack Brabham. He

was hit from behind off the line by his team-mate and insisted on pitting for a damage inspection, unwilling to risk his life. He finished the race third, but otherwise would probably have won both the race and the championship.

It was his last competitive season. Wanting to return to Britain, he was obliged to take drives in inferior cars, and he retired at the end of 1961.

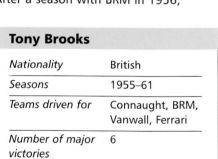

▶ Tony Brooks in his Ferrari during practice for the 1959 Italian Grand Prix. Clutch failure at the start of the race lost him a likely victory in the World Championship that year. He never came so close again.

David Bruce-Brown

As one of the stars of American racing, Bruce-Brown was recruited by the visiting European teams in the 1910 and 1911 American Grand Prize races. Against the cream of American and European racing combined, he won both times for Benz and Fiat respectively.

Highly impressed by his speed and intelligence, Fiat brought him over to Europe to compete in the 1912 French Grand Prix. He was leading the race against the Peugeot of Georges Boillot when he retired.

Commonly hailed as the best driver in the world at this time, he was killed during practice for the 1912 Vanderbilt Cup in Milwaukee.

David Bruce-Brown	
Nationality	American
Seasons	1910–12
Teams driven for	Benz, Fiat
Number of major victories	2

▲ David Bruce-Brown at the wheel of his Benz, at the Savannah Grand Prix, 1910.

▼ Bruce-Brown in the 1911 Vanderbilt Cup. He was killed in this event the following year.

Jenson Button

▼ Jenson Button in the Williams-BMW FW22 at the Japanese Grand Prix, Suzuka, in 2000.

Button burst onto the Formula One scene in sensational fashion in 2000 when, as a 20-year old, he was plucked from the junior ranks of racing to drive in Formula One for the mighty Williams-BMW team. By finishing sixth in Brazil 2000, his second race for the team, he became the youngest British Formula One driver ever to score a world championship point. He went on to several more stunning performances during his debut year, including out-qualifying Michael Schumacher on his first visit to the Belgian Grand Prix.

Despite generally out-performing his Williams team-mate, Ralf Schumacher, in the latter stages of the 2000 season, Button was moved aside at Williams to make way for Juan Pablo Montoya in 2001. The Colombian was already on a long term contract with Williams and Button had been used as a stand-in.

Nonetheless, it had enabled him to show his talent at the highest level, and he transferred across to the Renault team for the next two seasons. In 2003, he drove alongside Jacques Villeneuve at BAR-Honda and proceeded to out-perform the former world champion. He led both the American and Japanese Grands Prix. Button remains Britain's brightest Formula One prospect.

Jenson Button

Nationality	British
Seasons	2000–present
Teams driven for	Williams, Renault BAR
Number of major victories	0

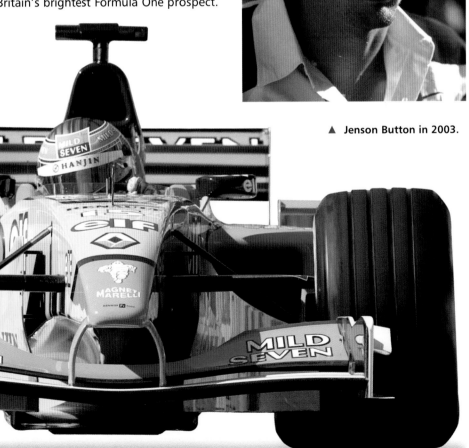
▼ Jenson Button in the Renault F1 R202 at the Monaco Grand Prix, 2002.

▲ Jenson Button in 2003.

Rudolf Caracciola

One of the all-time great Grand Prix drivers, Caracciola's career was intertwined with Mercedes in the 1920s and 1930s. He first made his reputation with some astonishing Grand Prix drives in the hopelessly heavy and unsuitable SSK sports car. With this he fought for victory in the first Monaco Grand Prix of 1929; twice he took the car to victory in the German Prix around the tortuous Nürburgring.

When Mercedes could offer him no racing programme for 1932, Caracciola switched to Alfa Romeo, where he instantly matched the speed of the legendary Tazio Nuvolari. He badly injured a leg in a practice accident at Monaco in 1933, and this came close to ending his career.

◀ Rudolf Caracciola in his Mercedes W163 during the 1939 French Grand Prix. He retired after hitting a wall.

He was tempted back by Mercedes as it re-entered Grand Prix racing under the Nazi regime in 1934. His silky touch had not deserted him and he was European Champion in 1935, '37 and '38. Rudi's greatest performances invariably came in the rain, where his uncanny feel led to the tag of "reinmeister".

After spending the duration of World War II in exile in Switzerland, Caracciola did not return to Grand Prix racing post-war. He died in 1959.

▲ Rudolf Caracciola, the European Champion of 1935, 1937 and 1938.

▶ Manfred von Brauchitsch and Caracciola, both driving for Mercedes, fight for the lead in the 1937 Monaco Grand Prix.

Rudolf Caracciola

Nationality	German
Seasons	1926–39
Teams driven for	Mercedes, Alfa Romeo
Number of major victories	17

François Cevert

C evert was being groomed by Ken Tyrrell as Jackie Stewart's heir, ready to take over as Tyrrell's lead driver after Stewart retired. With his talent, film star looks, intelligence and charm, he looked set to be a major star. He had spent three seasons under the combined tutelage of the two masters and looked set to be one of the elite of Formula One drivers. But in qualifying for the 1973 American Grand Prix – ironically due to be Stewart's final race – Cevert was killed attempting to secure pole position. Jackie withdrew, and the rest of the Formula One world mourned with him.

Cevert benefited from Elf's drive to promote young French talent. After winning a scholarship with the Winfield Racing School in 1968, he had proved very quick in Formula Three and

Formula Two, and he made his Formula One debut with the Elf-sponsored Tyrrell team in 1970. At the end of 1971, he won the American Grand Prix. In 1973, he dutifully followed Stewart home on three occasions, though the Scot later confided he believed Cevert could have passed him had he chosen to.

▲ François Cevert celebrates his first and only Grand Prix victory at Watkins Glen, USA, in 1971. It was the scene of his death two years later.

▼ Cevert at Montjuich Park, Spain, in 1973, where he finished second to his mentor, Jackie Stewart.

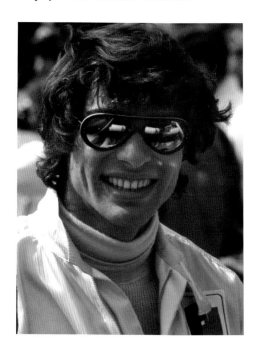

▲ Cevert in 1972: his film star looks belied talent and determination. A very bright future looked assured.

François Cevert

Nationality	French
Seasons	1970–73
Teams driven for	Tyrrell
Number of major victories	1

Fernand Charron

his French former cycle racer was the most successful of the first ever generation of racing drivers. Employed by Panhard, he made his reputation by winning the two biggest events of 1898, the Marseilles–Nice and the Paris–Amsterdam–Paris races.

Fast and daring, his British rival Charles Jarrott said of him: "Dare-devil, dashing and full of the winning spirit, his wins were hard-fought and hard-won. Without being what is ordinarily called nervous, he was nevertheless a mass of nerves, and he received little assistance from his physique to carry him through the strain and stress of driving a racing car at full speed throughout the long day. He is slightly built, small, dapper and quick as lightning when the occasion calls for quickness... As a really brilliant driver, Charron at his best had no equal."

▼ Charron in the Marseilles–Nice race of 1898. Winning this race helped to establish his reputation as a driver.

▲ Fernand Charron driving the Panhard in which he won the 565km (351-mile) Paris–Bordeaux race of 1899.

▼ Fernand Charron (right) driving a Panhard-Levassor in the Tour de France race of 1899.

HARRON MARSEILLE-NICE 1898

Fernand Charron

Nationality	French
Seasons	1897–1901
Teams driven for	Panhard
Number of major victories	4

Louis Chiron

▼ Chiron established himself as a frontline Grand Prix driver in Bugatti's type 35 model.

One of the major stars of Grand Prix racing in the late 1920s and 1930s, Chiron continued driving in Formula One until the mid-1950s.

A native of Monte Carlo, his early career was synonymous with Bugatti. He first began winning major races for this constructor in 1928, though not until 1931 did he finally manage to win his home Grand Prix.

He later transferred across to Alfa Romeo and produced what was arguably his finest drive when he took his Alfa P3 to victory in the 1934 French Grand Prix against the faster cars of Mercedes and Auto Union.

He continued his career post-war, but not with the same degree of success. After retiring, he was asked by Monaco's Prince Rainier to run the Monaco Grand Prix. He did so until his death in 1979, aged 78.

Louis Chiron	
Nationality	French
Seasons	1928–58
Teams driven for	Bugatti, Alfa Romeo, Mercedes, Talbot, Lancia
Number of major victories	14

◄ Chiron, here in his role of running the Monaco Grand Prix, talks to Juan Manuel Fangio.

▼ Chiron in a Scuderia-Ferrari Alfa Romeo P3 in 1934.

Jim Clark

The greatest driver of his era, Clark was World Champion in 1963 and 1965 and, at the time of his death in 1968, he had won more Grands Prix than anyone in the sport's history. He drove for Lotus throughout his Formula One career.

A Scottish farmer, he was adopted as a protégé by amateur racing driver Ian Scott-Watson. His early successes came in a variety of saloons and sports cars in local club racing. The break into the big time came after testing a Lotus Formula Two car at Brands Hatch, where he was trading times with the team's Formula One star Graham Hill. Lotus boss Colin Chapman was stunned when he subsequently learned that this was Clark's first ever drive in a single-seater.

Clark subsequently became a works Lotus Formula Two driver, and within a few months was making his Formula One debut in Holland in 1960. Chapman and Clark came to form a very close relationship, and as each man was a genius in their respective fields of design and driving, phenomenal success followed. As well as winning in Formula One, they also took the American racing world by storm with victory in the 1965 Indy 500.

Clark was 32 and at the height of his powers when he was killed in a Formula Two race at Hockenheim on 7 April 1968.

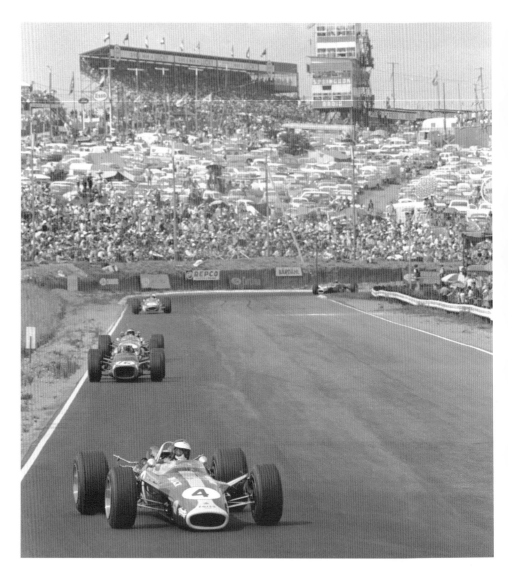

Jim Clark	
Nationality	British
Seasons	1960–68
Teams driven for	Lotus
Number of major victories	25

▲ Jim Clark dominating his final Grand Prix at South Africa in 1968.

▶ Jim Clark, World Drivers' Champion of 1963 and 1965.

▼ Clark gives the Lotus 25 its debut at the 1962 Dutch Grand Prix. He would win two world titles with this car and its derivative.

Peter Collins

◀ Collins stayed loyal to Ferrari from 1956 until his demise in 1958. He was a firm favourite of Enzo Ferrari.

C ollins' place in motorsport folklore was guaranteed when he gave up his chance of winning the 1956 World Championship by handing his car over to title rival and team-mate Juan Manuel Fangio in the final round. In what was a cruel twist of fate, he was denied any subsequent challenge for the crown, suffering a fatal accident during the 1958 German Grand Prix.

Collins was part of a new generation of British talent to emerge from that country's pioneering Formula 500 Championship. After a few promising runs for a variety of British teams from 1954 to 1955, his big chance came when he was signed by Ferrari for 1956. He won the Belgian and French Grand Prix that year and would almost certainly have taken the crown were it not for his act of supreme sportsmanship at Monza in the season finale.

He stayed at Ferrari in company with his close friend Mike Hawthorn for the rest of his time. Two weeks after winning the 1958 British Grand Prix, he was chasing Tony Brooks' race-leading Vanwall at the Nürburgring when his car left the road and overturned.

Peter Collins

Nationality	British
Seasons	1952–58
Teams driven for	HWM, Vanwall, Owen, Maserati, Ferrari
Number of major victories	3

◀ Peter Collins was just 20 years old when he made his Grand Prix debut, in 1952, and only 26 when he was killed.

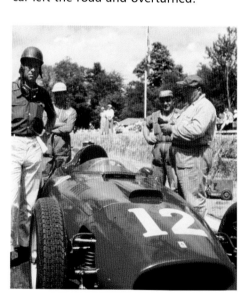

▲ Peter Collins with his Ferrari in 1957. Ferrari were not fully competitive that year, and Collins' best finishes were third in France and Germany.

▶ Peter Collins in his Mercedes at Targa Florio in 1955. He was beaten by team-mate Stirling Moss after suffering an accident.

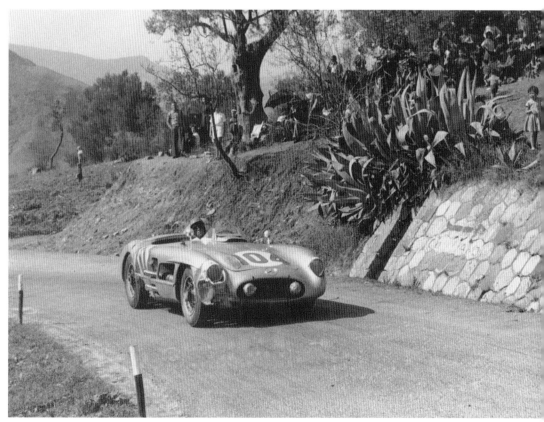

David Coulthard

The Scot's big career break came under the tragic circumstances of Ayrton Senna's death in 1994. As Williams' test driver, Coulthard took over the seat of the legendary Brazilian and established himself as a regular Grand Prix winner. His first victory came in 1995 in Portugal.

After beginning in karting, Coulthard served an apprenticeship in the British junior categories. He was competing in the European Formula 3000 Championship when his Formula One chance came. After taking four consecutive pole positions for Williams at the end of 1995, he switched to McLaren.

Initially, this was a backward step in terms of competitiveness, but he began his winning sequence for his new team with victory in Australia in 1997. The McLarens of 1998 and 1999 were the fastest cars but Coulthard was outshone by team-mate Mika Häkkinen. He mounted a serious title challenge to Michael Schumacher in 2001 but by this time the Ferraris had gained a performance advantage over McLaren. He continued to win races for McLaren through 2002 and 2003 and has served the team for longer than any other driver in its 35-year history.

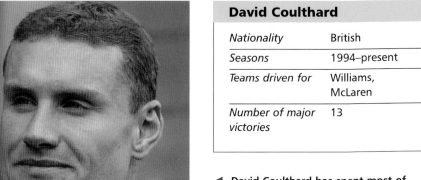

◄ David Coulthard in his Williams FW17 at the Spanish Grand Prix, Barcelona, in 1995. It was his first full season of Formula One.

David Coulthard

Nationality	British
Seasons	1994–present
Teams driven for	Williams, McLaren
Number of major victories	13

◄ David Coulthard has spent most of his Formula One career with McLaren after getting his first break with Williams.

▼ Coulthard took a great victory at Monaco in 2002. Here, he is chased by Juan Pablo Montoya and Michael Schumacher, neither of whom could break his defence.

Arthur Duray

Born in New York but a resident of France, Duray was one of the top drivers of the era of the sport before World War I. He enjoyed a long career that stretched from the turn of the 20th century to the late 1920s, though his halcyon days were with de Dietrich in 1905–07.

After establishing the land speed record at 134.31km/h (83.46mph) in 1903 for Gobron-Brille, Duray began racing with that company. De Dietrich then recruited him and they won the 1906 Circuit des Ardennes together.

After de Dietrich withdrew from the sport in 1912, Duray was left without a top drive but, undeterred, he continued in the small car class. He scored a stunning second place in the 1913 Indianapolis 500, having led for much of the distance, in a 3-litre Peugeot that was 2.5 litres down on the rest of the field. After the war, he continued racing in the voiturette and sports car categories, and continued to set speed records before his retirement in 1928.

▲ Arthur Duray in 1908.

◄ Arthur Duray, with de Dietrich emblem, at the 1907 Moscow–St Petersburg race.

▼ Arthur Duray in the Alcyon voiturette (small car) in the 1912 French Grand Prix. He continued in this class into the 1920s.

Arthur Duray

Nationality	French
Seasons	1903–14
Teams driven for	Gobron-Brille, de Dietrich, Delage, Peugeot
Number of major victories	1

Juan Manuel Fangio

This Argentinian legend was a five-time World Champion in the 1950s, and was commonly referred to as "El Maestro". His amazing Grand Prix career began when he was already in his late 30s, and he won his final title at the age of 46.

Hailing from a modest family background in Balcarce, his early racing exploits were on dirt roads in saloon cars, partly financed by whip-rounds among the people of his village. He quickly established a huge reputation in his homeland, but it was not until the leading European teams and drivers of the day visited Argentina for an off-season mini-series in 1948 that the phenomenon of Fangio was revealed to the wider world.

Jean-Pierre Wimille was acknowledged as the world's finest driver at that time. In the Rosario Grand Prix, he and Fangio were matched in identical Gordinis. They staged a superb duel. Wimille won but only after Fangio's car had begun to lose power. Fangio took the consolation of fastest lap. Afterwards, Wimille paid tribute to his rival and rightly predicted that great things awaited him.

The Argentinian Motor Club paid for a national team that included Fangio to race in European events in 1949. His form in the club's Maserati proved beyond all doubt his stunning

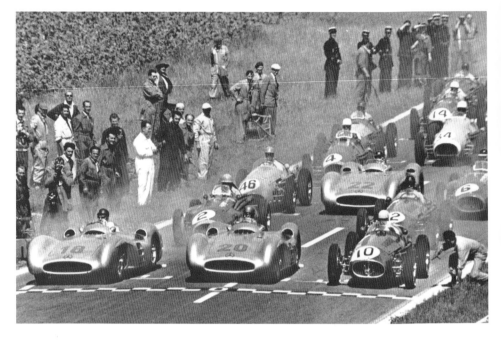

▲ **Fangio (18) starts the 1954 French Grand Prix in pole position, ahead of Karl Kling (20).**

Juan Manuel Fangio	
Nationality	Argentinian
Seasons	1949–58
Teams driven for	Alfa Romeo, Maserati, Mercedes, Ferrari
Number of major victories	24

speed, leading to his recruitment by Alfa-Romeo for the 1950 season.

Only unreliability kept him from victory in the inaugural World Championship that year, but he was a dominant champion in 1951. A neck-breaking accident kept him out for most of 1952 but he was back in his winning stride by 1953. He then won four successive world titles, a record that lasted 46 years. He retired in 1958 and returned to his homeland, where he ran a Mercedes-Benz dealership until his death in 1995.

◄ **Fangio became a legend through his exploits in the 1950s, when he won five world titles in eight years.**

▶ **Juan Manuel Fangio winning the International Trophy of 1951 at Silverstone for Alfa Romeo.**

Giuseppe Farina

Farina was already 44 years old when, in 1950, he won the inaugural World Championship. As a highly promising newcomer in the 1930s, his best years were probably lost to the war.

Farina had qualified to become a doctor of political science when at 26 years old he began his racing career. At Maserati he was taken under the wing of Tazio Nuvolari, but he really began to shine in voiturette racing with Alfa Romeo before the war intervened.

After a spell with Ferrari, he moved back to Alfa after the war in the new Formula One category. As a driver in the fastest car, he was well placed when the World Championship was inaugurated. His only competition for the title was team-mate Juan Manuel Fangio, whom he defeated through a superior finishing record. He won races in subsequent seasons with Ferrari, but retired at the end of 1955, having been troubled by leg burns incurred the previous year. He was killed in a road accident in 1966, while driving to the French Grand Prix.

◄ The 1950 World Championship title was the culmination of a long career for Giuseppe Farina.

▼ Farina became the sport's first World Champion with three victories in 1950.

▼ Farina winning the very first race of the World Championship at Silverstone in 1950.

Giuseppe Farina

Nationality	Italian
Seasons	1933–55
Teams driven for	Maserati, Alfa Romeo, Ferrari
Numer of major victories	7

Emerson Fittipaldi

By moving from his native Brazil to race in Europe to further his career, and then becoming World Champion in 1972 and 1974, Emerson Fittipaldi blazed a trail that countless South American drivers have followed ever since.

The son of a sports journalist, Emerson raced karts from an early age, along with his elder brother Wilson. He arrived in Britain in 1968 to race in the junior Formula Ford category, and proved an instant sensation. Lotus' Colin Chapman shrewdly signed him to drive the team's Formula Three and Formula Two cars, and by 1970 he was making his Formula One debut.

In fairy-tale fashion, he won his fifth Grand Prix, this result in America ensuring that Lotus' recently-deceased Jochen Rindt became a posthumous World Champion. After a sequence of victories, he became the sport's youngest-ever World Champion in 1972, aged 25. He joined McLaren for 1974 and promptly won another title.

Surprisingly, he left McLaren at the end of 1975 to drive for the Brazilian Copersucar team that had been founded by his brother Wilson. It proved a frustrating venture, and in five years of trying Emerson never did find success with the cars. He retired for a time before making a glorious comeback in Indycar racing, winning two Indy 500s before his final retirement from motorsport in 1996.

Emerson Fittipaldi

Nationality	Brazilian
Seasons	1970–80
Teams driven for	Lotus, McLaren, Fittipaldi
Number of major victories	14

▲ Fittipaldi's final podium came with third place in the 1980 USA West Grand Prix – from 24th on the grid.

▼ Fittipaldi's victory at Watkins Glen in 1970 ensured that his late team-mate Jochen Rindt took the world title.

▲ Fittipaldi stands on top of the podium after his fifth Grand Prix, the USA, in 1970.

José Froilán González

The burly Argentinian, known as the "Pampas Bull", won Ferrari's first ever championship-stature Grand Prix, when he beat his friend Fangio's Alfa at Silverstone in 1951.

Fangio was instrumental in getting González an opportunity in Europe in 1950, and his form in a privately-run Maserati brought him his recruitment to Ferrari the following year. After a spell alongside Fangio at Maserati, he returned to Ferrari in 1954, again winning the British Grand Prix and finishing runner-up in the World Championship that season.

At the end of the year, he was injured in a sports car race and niggles from this led to his retirement from regular competition, though he continued to appear at his home Grand Prix until 1960. He concentrated thereafter on his garage business.

Froilan Gonzalez	
Nationality	Argentinian
Seasons	1950–60
Teams driven for	Maserati, Ferrari
Number of major victories	2

◀ Froilián González at the Argentine Grand Prix in 1973, 13 years after his retirement.

▼ *(right)* Froilán González during the 1954 German Grand Prix in his Ferrari.

▼ *(bottom)* Silverstone and the start of the 1951 British Grand Prix, with González (12) racing head to head with Juan Manuel Fangio's Alfa Romeo. González won the race, and Fangio finished in second place.

▼ *(left)* Froilán González on his way to the first Championship-status Grand Prix win for Ferrari at Silverstone in 1951.

Dan Gurney

▼ Gurney took his first Grand Prix victory at Rouen in 1962. It stands as the only such win for the Porsche marque.

In a 12-year Formula One career that spanned spells at Ferrari, BRM, Porsche, Brabham and his own Eagle team, the American Gurney frequently displayed outstanding talent, but was never able to create the right circumstances for a title bid.

The son of an opera singer, he began racing sports cars in California in the early 1950s. The American Ferrari importer Luigi Chinetti was instrumental in getting Gurney a chance with the Ferrari sports car team in Europe in 1958. This opportunity led to his Grand Prix graduation with the team the following year. He made a great impression, running at the front in just his second race.

Uneasy about the politics within Ferrari, he moved to BRM for 1960, but the car proved less competitive than hoped, and this led him to accept an offer to lead Porsche's new Formula One effort for 1961. He gave the team its only Grand Prix victory at France in 1962, having narrowly lost out in the same race in 1961. The disappointing form of the cars led to the German company's withdrawal at the end of 1962, and this left Gurney to hook up with Jack Brabham, who was in the throes of establishing his own team.

Gurney, rather than double World Champion Brabham, proved to be the cutting edge of the driving squad, and in 1964 he gave them their first victory, in France. He won again in Mexico that year, but at the end of a relatively

Dan Gurney	
Nationality	American
Seasons	1959–70
Teams driven for	Ferrari, BRM, Porsche, Brabham, Eagle, McLaren
Number of major victories	4

▼ Two years after his success for Porsche, Gurney gave the Brabham team its first win.

barren 1965, he left to pursue the dream of creating his own team, Eagle. This cost him a real chance of the 1966 World Championship, as Brabhams proved the dominant cars that year.

Gurney won in Belgium in 1967 in the Eagle, but thereafter the car was left behind by the new DFV-powered machines and Gurney's interest in Formula One waned. He drove his last Grand Prix in 1970, as a stand-in at McLaren, and went on to enjoy considerable success as a team owner in Indy car racing.

▲ Dan Gurney celebrates his victory at Rouen in France in 1964.

Mika Häkkinen

The furiously fast Finn came back from near-death in 1995 to win the World Championships of 1998 and 1999 with McLaren-Mercedes.

Managed by former World Champion Keke Rosberg after early years in karting and Formula Ford, he was backed by Marlboro to pursue his career in Britain where he became Formula Three Champion in 1990. Lotus' Peter Collins had a sharp eye for new talent, and he signed Hakkinen for 1991. He performed with much promise, but the team's glory days were over. For 1993, he accepted a role as test driver with McLaren, reasoning that he needed to show his pace in a top car even if it meant not racing in the short term.

When McLaren dropped Michael Andretti near the end of the season,

Mika Häkkinen	
Nationality	Finnish
Seasons	1991–2001
Teams driven for	Lotus, McLaren
Number of major victories	20

after a series of disappointing performances, Häkkinen stepped up to replace him. In a sensational performance, he outqualified his team-mate, the great Ayrton Senna, and his future was seemingly assured.

In qualifying for the 1995 Australian Grand Prix, a puncture-induced accident left him critically injured, and only an

emergency tracheotomy, track-side, saved his life. Remarkably, he seemed to have lost none of his speed when he returned for the start of 1996.

The breakthrough came at the end of 1997 in Jerez, though Häkkinen's victory there was gifted to him by Williams' Jacques Villeneuve, as thanks for McLaren co-operation in not attacking him in the early stages of the race as he fought for the world title with Michael Schumacher.

It was the prelude to a devastating run of victories in the superb McLaren-Mercedes of 1998 and 1999. Häkkinen only narrowly lost out on a third title in 2000. He retired at the end of 2001, though left the door open for a future possible return. In 2002, he announced his retirement was permanent.

▲ *(right)* Mika Häkkinen in the Lotus 102B at the rain-shortened Australian Grand Prix.

▲ *(left)* Häkkinen at the Melbourne Grand Prix in 2001. It was here he made the decision to retire from Formula One.

▶ Häkkinen driving his McLaren MP4-14 to victory in the Brazilian Grand Prix at Interlagos in 1999.

Mike Hawthorn

Hawthorn became the first British World Champion when he took the title for Ferrari in 1958. He immediately retired from what was then a lethally dangerous sport, but ironically was killed in a road accident just a few months later.

After a lightning quick rise through British club racing in the early 1950s, aided by his former bike-racing father, Hawthorn found himself on the international stage in 1952, when Formula Two was made the World Championship category. Some great performances in a Cooper-Bristol caught the eye of Enzo Ferrari, who signed him for 1953. In the French Grand Prix of that year, Hawthorn scored his first victory after a stirring wheel-to-wheel battle with Juan Manuel Fangio's Maserati.

It would be another five years before Hawthorn was once again in a fully competitive Ferrari, and although he won only the French Grand Prix in 1958, he scored highly everywhere and secured the title in the final round – with some help from team-mate Phil Hill, who moved aside to hand him second place.

After retiring to his garage business, Hawthorn fatally crashed his road car near Guildford in January 1959.

◀ Blonde and dashing, Hawthorn captured the public's imagination.

Mike Hawthorn	
Nationality	British
Seasons	1952–58
Teams driven for	Ferrari, Vanwall, BRM
Number of major victories	3

▼ Mike Hawthorn takes over the car of Ferrari team-mate José Froilán González on lap 16 of the 1954 German Grand Prix.

▲ Hawthorn in the Ferrari model 246 at the Monaco Grand Prix. The car won him the 1958 World Championship title.

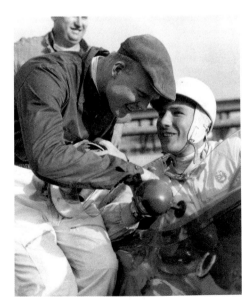

▲ Hawthorn and Stirling Moss battled hard over the destiny of the 1958 world title. Hawthorn narrowly won.

Damon Hill

The 1996 World Champion Hill graduated from the role of test driver to racer for the mighty Williams-Renault team, following the departure of Nigel Mansell. It was a gifted opportunity, and it led to a fruitful association for all concerned.

The son of double World Champion Graham Hill, Damon began racing on motorbikes, and did not progress to cars until he was well into his 20s. A front runner in British Formula Ford and Formula Three racing, he was competing in Formula 3000 in 1991 when he was offered the chance by Williams to test-drive for Formula One.

He made his Grand Prix debut with the uncompetitive Brabham team in 1992. It proved useful experience for when he gained his first big break with Williams the following season. Alongside the great Alain Prost, he acquitted himself well, and he won his first Grand Prix in Hungary.

In 1994, he stepped up as team leader following the death of Prost's replacement, Ayrton Senna. His nemesis proved to be Benetton's Michael Schumacher, and the championship battle distilled into a final round shoot-out between the two men. Schumacher and Hill pulled well away from the rest in Adelaide, and Hill pounced when Schumacher was slowed after an off-track moment, but the German turned in on him, damaging Hill's suspension. With both out, Hill had lost the title. He was comfortably beaten by Schumacher in 1995, but put this to rights in 1996. With his new team-mate Jacques Villeneuve as his only serious rival, Hill clinched the title in Japan.

Controversially, Williams dropped Hill for 1997, leaving him to drive for the smaller Arrows team with which he came within an ace of winning the Grand Prix in Hungary. For 1998, he switched to Jordan, winning the team's first – and his 22nd – Grand Prix, at Belgium. He retired after a disappointing 1999 season.

► **Hill taking his Williams FW18 to a dominant victory in the 1996 Brazilian Grand Prix.**

Damon Hill

Nationality	British
Seasons	1992–99
Teams driven for	Brabham, Williams, Arrows, Jordan
Number of major victories	22

▲ *(Top)* **Damon Hill making his Grand Prix debut in the outclassed Brabham BT60B at the 1992 British Grand Prix.**

◄ **Hill in 1998 when he drove for Jordan and gave them their first Grand Prix win.**

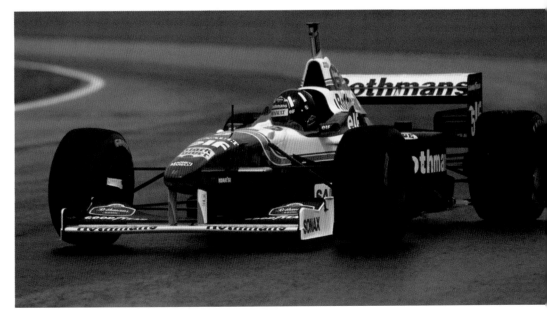

Graham Hill

The World Champion of 1962 and 1968 became a folk hero of the sport for his gritty determination and winning public persona. He retired from the driving seat in 1975 to devote himself to running his own team, but was killed piloting his light aircraft in November of that year.

After talking himself into a mechanic's job with Lotus in the mid-1950s, Hill got himself into the driving seat of the team's Formula Two and sports cars. When Lotus graduated to Formula One in 1958, Hill was one of the drivers. It wasn't until he switched to BRM in 1960, though, that he began to show some form; he looked set to win a superb victory in that year's British Grand Prix, but spun it away. For 1962, BRM had produced a powerful new V8 engine, and with this he scored his first race successes, culminating in his first world title at the end of that season.

He stayed at BRM, a regular race winner, until transferring back to Lotus for 1967. In between, he won the 1966 Indianapolis 500. The new Cosworth DFV engine in the Lotus 49 gave Hill a highly competitive but unreliable

▲ Graham Hill in 1973.

▼ Graham Hill in the BRM P48 at the British Grand Prix, Silverstone, 1960. He stormed up the field after stalling on the grid, but retired from the lead late in the race after a spin caused by brake failure.

Graham Hill	
Nationality	British
Seasons	1958–75
Teams driven for	Lotus, BRM, Brabham, Hill
Number of major victories	14

1967 season. When his friend and team-mate Jim Clark was killed early in 1968, Hill pulled the team back together with some great performances, and he clinched his second title in the final round. He won his fifth Monaco Grand Prix in 1969, but badly injured his legs at Watkins Glen. He never regained his Formula One form subsequently, but battled on for a few more years, and won the 1972 Le Mans 24 Hours sports car race for Matra.

He was returning from a test session with his team when he crashed his plane in fog as he attempted to land at Elstree near London. Five team members, including his young driver Tony Brise, died with him.

Phil Hill

America's first World Champion, Hill took the title with Ferrari in 1961. The son of a California postmaster, Hill began racing sports cars in the early 1950s, working on and preparing them himself. Ever-improving form brought him to the attention of Ferrari importer Luigi Chinetti who got Hill a sports car chance with the Ferrari works team. He enjoyed considerable success here, but his constant badgering for a Formula One chance took a long time to be answered.

In his first Formula One drive for the team, at Monza in 1958, he took third place and fastest lap. At the next event in Morocco, he outpaced his team-mate and that year's World Champion, Mike Hawthorn. Such an impressive start ensured a permanent place in the Formula One team.

He took fourth place in the 1959 Championship, but suffered in 1960 through Ferrari's front-engined policy. The following year, the Ferrari 156 was by far the fastest car of the season, and Hill became locked in battle for the title with his team-mate Wolfgang von Trips. Into the penultimate round at Monza

▲ Race winner Phil Hill (Ferrari) at the Italian Grand Prix, Monza, 1961.

▼ Phil Hill in the Ferrari 156 leads team-mate Wolfgang von Trips at the Belgian Grand Prix, 1961. Hill won the race, and Trips came second in a Ferrari 1-2-3-4.

Phil Hill	
Nationality	American
Seasons	1958–66
Teams driven for	Ferrari, ATS, Cooper, Eagle
Number of major victories	3

there was little to split them, but von Trips crashed to his death. Hill won the race and the title in the most tragic of circumstances.

Hill never approached such heights again in Formula One. Ferrari was overwhelmed by the British teams in 1962, though Hill performed superbly. A move to the new ATS team for 1963 proved disastrous, and his last full season was with Cooper in 1964. He enjoyed further sports car success – having won Le Mans three times – before retirement at the end of 1966. He later devoted himself to his classic car restoration business in California.

Denny Hulme

▼ Denny Hulme took his only pole position at the South Africa Grand Prix in 1973, when he gave the McLaren M23 its debut drive.

New Zealand's first, and to date only, World Drivers' Champion, Denny Hulme took the title for the Brabham team in only his second full Formula One season.

After winning a "Driver To Europe" award in his home country, Hulme served his racing apprenticeship with Brabham, driving their Formula Two cars as well as being the truck driver. He got occasional runs in the Formula One car in 1965, and was promoted to the seat full-time the following year, after Dan Gurney left the team.

His role was one of back up to Jack Brabham in 1967. But frequently "improvements" made to the team leader's car proved unreliable, and Hulme was invariably there to pick up the pieces, and ultimately the title. He moved to fellow countryman Bruce McLaren's team for 1968, where he remained until the end of his Formula One career in 1974. He challenged for the Championship again in 1968, for McLaren, and was a regular race-winner until he left Formula One. He came out of retirement to race touring cars in Australia in the 1980s and early 1990s, and it was while competing in the Bathurst race in 1992 that he suffered a fatal heart attack. He was 55.

Denny Hulme	
Nationality	New Zealand
Seasons	1965–74
Teams driven for	Brabham, McLaren
Number of major victories	8

▼ Hulme driving the Brabham BT7 in his Grand Prix debut at the 1967 Monaco Grand Prix. He finished in eighth place.

▲ Third place in the 1967 Mexican Grand Prix secured Hulme's world title from his team-mate Jack Brabham.

James Hunt

World Champion of 1976 after a dramatic battle with Niki Lauda, Hunt was a controversial figure from the beginning of his Formula One career in 1973 to the end in 1979. In between he produced some brilliant drives for Hesketh and McLaren.

In the junior categories, he established a reputation as being quick but accident-prone, and was nicknamed "Hunt the Shunt". After being dropped by the March Formula Three team, he was picked up by Lord Hesketh's eccentric new team.

They initially planned to tackle Formula Two together in 1973, but after realizing they could compete in Formula One for a little more money by buying a car from March, they did just that. Hunt soon began to surprise the Formula One paddock with his speed, and within a few races was running near the front. In the American Grand Prix, he chased victor Ronnie Peterson hard all the way, and crossed the line just fractions of a second behind. The March was replaced by a Hesketh design in 1974, and Hunt won the non-championship International Trophy Formula One race at Silverstone. In 1975, he won the Dutch Grand Prix in a brilliant drive, during which he held off the faster Ferrari of Niki Lauda.

It was the Austrian with whom Hunt was locked in combat after he moved to McLaren for 1976, with Hunt clinching the title by just one point in the final round at Japan. He won three more times in 1977, but the competitiveness of McLaren was on the wane. He switched to Wolf for 1979, but the car proved no more competitive than the McLaren, and he retired part way through the season. He died in 1993, aged 46, after suffering a heart attack.

◄ **James Hunt: daring, dashing, all-British hero of the 1970s.**

▲ **James Hunt winning the 1976 British Grand Prix at Brands Hatch. He was later disqualified from the race.**

James Hunt	
Nationality	British
Seasons	1973–79
Teams driven for	Hesketh, McLaren, Wolf
Number of major victories	10

▼ **When the 1979 Wolf WR7 – here, at Argentina – proved uncompetitive, Hunt decided to hang up his helmet.**

Jacky Ickx

Twice runner-up in the World Championship, the Belgian Ickx was one of the fastest drivers around in the late 1960s and early 1970s.

He graduated from motorcycle racing to Formula Three and touring cars with Ken Tyrrell. A move to Formula Two followed. At that time the German Grand Prix on the 22.5km (14-mile) Nürburgring circuit allowed for Formula Two cars to join Formula Ones. Ickx caused a sensation by qualifying third-quickest for the 1967 event, faster than Jackie Stewart, John Surtees and Jack Brabham, all of whom were in Formula One cars with engines 1.4 litres bigger than that in Ickx's Formula Two Matra.

This performance brought a Ferrari drive for 1968. He won that year's French Grand Prix in the rain, and his reputation as one of the greatest wet weather drivers took hold. A switch to Brabham for 1969 gave him second place in the World Championship, and then it was back to Ferrari for 1970, where he was the only man to threaten Jochen Rindt's posthumous title.

Ferrari were by then producing ever-less competitive cars, and this allowed Ickx to grab only the occasional victory before leaving the team in 1973. A disappointing spell with Lotus led to him leaving Formula One to concentrate on sports cars, where he continued to be highly successful. He retired in 1985, having won the Le Mans 24 Hours six times.

Jacky Ickx

Nationality	Belgian
Seasons	1967–79
Teams driven for	Cooper, Ferrari, Brabham, Lotus, Wolf, Ensign, Ligier
Major victories	8

▲ Ickx in 1970, when he was in real contention for the world title.

◄ Ickx's Ferrari leads Peterson (March) and team-mate Clay Regazzoni at the German Grand Prix in 1972.

Alan Jones

T he first of many to win a World title with the Williams team, the Australian Jones drove Formula One cars from 1975 to 1981 before a brief retirement. He returned in 1985–86, but without the same level of success.

The son of Melbourne racing star Stan Jones, he moved to Britain in the early 1970s and became a front-runner in the British Formula Three and Formula 5000 categories. He drove for a series of small, underfunded Formula One teams in 1975 and 1976, but despite a race-leading drive for Surtees in the 1976 race of champions he entered 1977 without a drive. It looked as though his Formula One career was over, but after the tragedy of Tom Pryce's death in the South African Grand Prix, Jones was rescued by the Shadow team. He drove several very strong races, culminating in a surprise victory in Austria.

This led to his recruitment by Frank Williams to drive the first Patrick Head-designed Williams for 1978. This proved a highly competitive machine, and Jones was challenging for victory in the 1978 USA West Grand Prix. Head's ground-effect FW07 of 1979 was even better and, in the latter half of that year, Jones took four victories. This was the build-up to his title-winning campaign of 1980. He drove some superb, aggressive races in 1981, still in the FW07, and bowed out with victory in the final race at Las Vegas, having announced his retirement.

He was tempted back by Arrows into a brief comeback in 1983, and a more serious one, by the new Ford-backed Beatrice team, in 1985. Although the Ross Brawn-designed car was good, its Ford V6 lacked horsepower and Jones was never a serious contender. He called it a day – along with the Beatrice team – at the end of 1986.

Alan Jones	
Nationality	Australian
Seasons	1975–86
Teams driven for	Hesketh, Hill, Surtees, Shadow, Williams, Arrows, Beatrice
Number of major victories	12

◄ Alan Jones on top of the podium for the first time at the Osterreichring in 1977.

▲ *(right)* Alan Jones took a surprise win for Shadow in the rain at Austria in 1977. It was this result that attracted him to Williams for 1978.

► Jones bowed out of Formula One for the first time in great style, winning the 1981 Las Vegas Grand Prix.

Niki Lauda

The three-time World Champion Lauda became one of the all-time legends of the sport when, in 1976, he made a comeback from being given the last rites on his deathbed to fourth place in the Italian Grand Prix in just a matter of weeks.

Lauda was recruited by Ferrari in 1974 as a promising newcomer who had shown well in the outclassed BRM of 1973. His technical adeptness and capacity for testing made him the perfect partner for Ferrari designer Mauro Forghieri, as they spent hour upon hour testing at Ferrari's new Fiorano test track. The hard work paid off as Lauda reeled off a great sequence of nine pole positions and took his first two victories.

In 1975, his Ferrari 312T dominated the Championship, with five wins. After beginning 1976 in similar fashion, he crashed in the early laps of the German Grand Prix, incurring critical lung damage as he lay unconscious in his burning car. After a remarkable comeback, he pulled out of the title-deciding Japanese Grand Prix, unwilling to risk his life in the blinding spray. This lost him the title to James Hunt.

He won back the title in 1977, and then walked out on Ferrari with two races still to go – an act of revenge for the lack of support he felt the team gave him in his 1976 comeback.

▲ Niki Lauda in the BRM P160E of 1973. It was his pace in this car that brought him to the attention of Ferrari.

Niki Lauda

Nationality	Austrian
Seasons	1971–85
Teams driven for	March, BRM, Ferrari, Brabham, McLaren
Number of major victories	25

▼ Lauda takes the lead from Andrea de Cesaris on his way to victory in the 1982 USA West Grand Prix at Long Beach.

He joined the Brabham team where he scored two victories in 1978, but at the penultimate race of 1979 he promptly retired, saying he was bored with driving round in circles.

After two years building up his airline business, he was tempted to return for 1982 by McLaren's Ron Dennis. He won on his third race back, and went on to victory in the 1984 World Championship. He retired permanently at the end of 1985.

▼ Lauda at Zolder, Belgium, in 1976, five races before his scarring accident, and the prelude to the bravest comeback of all time.

Vincenzo Lancia

The son of a wealthy country squire who had a soup-manufacturing empire, Lancia was a trainee with the Ceirano car company – which hired its workshop space from Lancia's father – when the company was taken over by Fiat at the turn of the 20th century. He had already made his competition debut in a small-time race with Ceirano, and was used by Fiat for similar events as well as being employed by them as a test driver.

When Fiat progressed to international racing, Lancia went with them. He soon established a reputation as a furiously fast competitor, but often his mechanical sympathy seemed to desert him and he would invariably retire from leading positions – often leaving victory to his team-mate Felice Nazzaro.

Whilst still in the employ of Fiat, he founded his own company, Lancia, to produce sporting road cars. His driving career at Fiat continued until 1910, after which he concentrated on the running of his company. He would preside over this and engineer many innovations until his death in 1937, aged 56. His son Gianni took over the car company which bore the family name and later took it into Grand Prix racing. Just like Vincenzo, the 1954–55 Lancia proved to be very fast but, ultimately, unreliable.

◄ Lancia at the French Grand Prix of 1906.

▼ *(left)* Vincenzo Lancia in 1907.

Vincenzo Lancia	
Nationality	Italian
Seasons	1900–10
Teams driven for	Fiat
Number of major victories	0

▼ Lancia winning the Florio Cup in a 75hp Fiat with an average speed of 115.70km/h (71.89mph) in 1904.

Emile Levassor

The winner of the first ever motorcar race, engineer Emile Levassor triumphed in the 1895 Paris–Bordeaux–Paris race in his Panhard-Levassor by over five hours.

As a partner in the former woodworking company, Panhard, he took it into car manufacture when a friend acquired the French commercial rights to the new Daimler engine. The engine was installed in a chassis more advanced than that of the Daimler, and this led to the car being the dominant force in the pioneer sport.

Levassor suffered an accident after hitting a dog during the 1896 Paris–Marseilles race. His car rolled, throwing him out, and although he was able to restart and finish the event in fourth place, the internal injuries he incurred proved fatal. He died the following year, aged 53. Motorsport's first hero had also become its first fatality.

▼ Emile Levassor.

◄ Emile Levassor, winner of the first true motor race, in 1895.

▼ Levassor is commemorated in stone at Porte Mallot near Paris.

Emile Levassor

Nationality	French
Seasons	1895–96
Teams driven for	Panhard
Number of major victories	1

Nigel Mansell

A dominant World Champion in 1992, Mansell's career was a Wurlitzer ride of high-drama and spine-tingling excitement.

He was a struggling Formula Three driver with a broken bone in his neck from a recent race accident when Lotus boss Colin Chapman invited him to test a Formula One car. Keeping his injury secret, Mansell did the test and performed well enough to be offered a test-driver role for the team in 1980. He made his race debut in Austria that year, sitting bathed in leaking petrol for many laps before the car eventually failed. He was signed as a full-time member of the race team in 1981, but his career received a setback with the death of Chapman in 1982.

Although Mansell was retained by the team, he no longer received the same treatment, and relations became strained with the new management. He was dominating the wet Monaco Grand Prix of 1984 when he made a mistake and crashed out. The following year he was replaced – Lotus signed Ayrton Senna – but Mansell's career was given a lifeline as he was recruited by Williams for 1985. Towards the end of the season, he made a breakthrough victory in front of his home crowd at Brands Hatch. He immediately followed it up with another, in South Africa.

His 1986 season was a fierce battle with new Williams team-mate Nelson Piquet, though both ultimately lost out

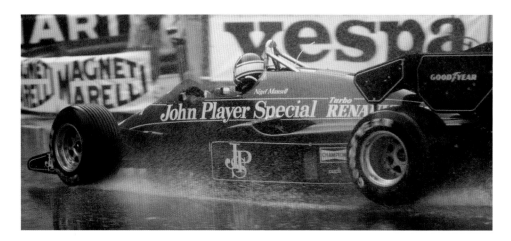

▲ **Nigel Mansell leading the 1984 Monaco Grand Prix in his Lotus 95T. He later crashed out of the race.**

Nigel Mansell	
Nationality	British
Seasons	1980–95
Teams driven for	Lotus, Williams, Ferrari, McLaren
Number of major victories	31

▼ **(left) Mansell: determination always saw him through. He was one of the most exciting performers the sport has seen.**

▼ **(right) Mansell leading the 1990 British Grand Prix. He announced his retirement after the race but later changed his mind.**

to Alain Prost. Mansell was on course for the title, with 19 laps to go in the final race, when a rear tyre exploded dramatically. He was again in title contention in 1987, but injured his back in practice for the penultimate race.

He joined Ferrari in 1989, and won his first race for them. He won a total of three races for the team, but left at the end of 1990 to rejoin Williams. After narrowly losing the 1991 title to McLaren's Ayrton Senna, Mansell wiped up in 1992 with the devastatingly fast active-ride Williams FW14B. Unable to agree terms for 1993, he headed for America, where he became CART Champion. He returned to Williams in 1994 as a stand-in, and won the Australian Grand Prix. His full Formula One comeback with McLaren in 1995 was aborted after just a few races as the car proved uncompetitive.

Guy Moll

T he Algerian driver Moll looked to have a brilliant career ahead of him after making an instant impact at the highest level of the sport, in the early 1930s.

A protégé of compatriot and Bugatti driver Marcel Lehoux, Moll finished second in the 1933 Pau Grand Prix, his first international competition. This brought him to the attention of Enzo Ferrari, who recruited him to drive Alfa Romeos alongside established stars, Achille Varzi and Louis Chiron.

Guy Moll	
Nationality	Algerian
Seasons	1933–34
Teams driven for	Alfa Romeo
Number of major victories	1

▼ Guy Moll, winner of the Monaco Grand Prix, in 1934. Enzo Ferrari is third from the top on the extreme left of the picture.

He instantly proved their match, and won the 1934 Monaco Grand Prix. For a virtial rookie, such performances bordered on miraculous.

He was fighting Mercedes driver Luigi Fagioli for victory at Pescara, in 1934, when he crashed trying to lap the Mercedes of Ernst Henne. He was thrown out of his car into a tree, suffering fatal injuries. Several decades later, Enzo Ferrari said he believed Moll would have proved himself to be one of the all-time great drivers had he lived.

Juan Pablo Montoya

▼ Montoya *(left)* and Michael Schumacher in one of several wheel-to-wheel battles: here, at Melbourne in 2002.

Since entering Formula One in 2001, the Colombian Montoya has established himself as one of the sport's most exciting performers.

After winning the 1998 European Formula 3000 Championship, Montoya transferred to American CART racing. He won the championship at his first attempt, astounding veterans of the series with his phenomenal car control and an ability to overtake in places never seen before. In 2000, he won the Indianapolis 500 at his first attempt.

The Williams Formula One team had put him on a long-term contract when he was still in Formula 3000, and for 2001 they decided it was time to bring him to Formula One. In Brazil, his third race, he created a sensation by overtaking Michael Schumacher, rubbing tyres, then pulling away to victory. Only the mistake of a lapped backmarker denied him. He finally won at Monza for the Italian Grand Prix. In 2002 he scored seven pole positions, and in 2003 was in contention for the World Championship until the penultimate round.

Juan Pablo Montoya

Nationality	Colombian
Seasons	2001–present
Teams driven for	Williams
Number of major victories	3

▼ Brazil 2001: Montoya makes his move inside Schumacher to take the lead, rubbing wheels along the way *(inset)*.

► Juan Pablo Montoya, a combative performer whose exciting driving style has captured imaginations.

Stirling Moss

From the time of Juan Manuel Fangio's retirement in 1958 to his own injury-induced retirement in 1962, Stirling Moss was widely recognized as the world's greatest driver. That he never won the world title was seen as an indictment of the Championship rather than any slur on his skills.

After establishing a big reputation in the British junior classes, Moss competed in his first Formula One season in 1954 with a privately-owned Maserati 250F. His form in this was so impressive that he was later given a drive with the works team. Only mechanical failure lost him that year's Italian Grand Prix. This led to his recruitment by Mercedes for the 1955 season, when he drove alongside the acknowledged master of Formula One, Fangio. Moss won the British Grand Prix, but to this day he is unsure whether Fangio allowed him to do so.

Following Mercedes' withdrawal, Moss rejoined Maserati, but it was his switch to the British Vanwall team in 1957 that brought him bigger success. Between 1957 and 1958 he won six Grands Prix for the team. His tally of four wins in 1958 compared to one for the World Champion, Mike Hawthorn.

Stirling Moss	
Nationality	British
Seasons	1951–62
Teams driven for	HWM, Connaught, Cooper, Maserati, Mercedes, Vanwall, Walker, BRP, Ferguson
Number of major victories	16

▼ Moss drove one of his greatest races in the under-powered Rob Walker Lotus 18 to win the Monaco Grand Prix in 1961.

◄ Stirling Moss, photographed at Silverstone in 1955.

After Vanwall's withdrawal, Moss spent most of the remainder of his career driving for privateer Rob Walker, first in a Cooper and latterly a Lotus. In 1961, he produced two of his greatest drives to win the Monaco and German Grands Prix against the faster Ferraris. Early in 1962 he suffered a big accident at a non-championship race at Goodwood, and his life hung in the balance for a while. Though he made a full recovery, he felt his incomparable skills had been impaired, and reluctantly retired, still in his early 30s. He remains a household name in retirement.

▼ Stirling Moss beats Mercedes team-mate Juan Manuel Fangio to the chequered flag in the 1955 British Grand Prix.

Felice Nazzaro

Nazzaro was one of the master drivers for a long period from the early-1900s to the early 1920s. His successes came almost exclusively with Fiat, for whom he later became competition director.

Like his compatriot Vincenzo Lancia, he was apprenticed to the Ceirano company at the turn of the century, but was retained when that company was bought out by Fiat. When Fiat moved into big-time international racing, Nazzaro immediately proved his class. His drives were a calculating blend of early race caution and searing speed when the occasion demanded it, and his finishing record was far superior to the more spectacular Lancia's. In 1907, he won all three major races of the season, and was still winning in 1922.

◄ A portrait of Felice Nazzaro in 1907 when he won all three major races of the season. He raced successfully until 1924.

▼ (left) Felice Nazzaro, in the 1913 French Grand Prix at Amiens. This was one of the few races in which he didn't drive for the Fiat marque.

Felice Nazzaro

Nationality	Italian
Seasons	1900–24
Teams driven for	Fiat, Itala
Number of major victories	5

In that year he took victory in the French Grand Prix, the same race in which his nephew, Biagio Nazzaro, was killed in another Fiat. He retired from the driving seat at the end of 1924, but remained with the company until his death in 1940.

▼ Nazzaro's Fiat came second at the Italian Grand Prix of 1922, on the new Monza track, but here he leads a Bugatti and a Diatto.

Tazio Nuvolari

till regarded by many as the greatest driver who has ever lived, Nuvolari's reign as a giant of the sport lasted from the late 1920s until the outbreak of World War II. Though his list of victories in Bugattis, Alfa Romeos, Maseratis and Auto Unions was long, it was his frequent giant-killing "impossible" victories against superior machinery that sealed his reputation.

Never interested in taking over the family farms, instead Tazio sold some of the land he had inherited to begin a career in motorcycle racing. He became a hero of that sport in the mid-1920s, his spectacular style in sharp contrast to the cool calculation of his arch rival, Achille Varzi.

The two drivers combined forces to form their own racing stable, in which to begin their car racing careers proper, though Nuvolari had already dabbled with four-wheel competition. Though they were both successful in their team of Bugattis, it was an uneasy relationship, and Varzi left after little more than a year.

▲ **Tazio Nuvolari c. 1933.**

▼ **Nuvolari in action for Alfa Romeo at the Monaco Grand Prix of 1932.**

Tazio Nuvolari	
Nationality	Italian
Seasons	1928–46
Teams driven for	Alfa Romeo, Bugatti, Maserati, Auto Union
Number of major victories	18

By the time Nuvolari received his first big break in a works Alfa Romeo, courtesy of Enzo Ferrari, he was already 37 years old. But it made no difference to his form, and he racked up one spectacular victory after another, often after stirring battles with Varzi.

The overwhelming superiority of the German cars from 1934 onwards left Nuvolari in uncompetitive machinery. Varzi, by contrast, had signed with Auto Union, and made it a stipulation that he would not drive alongside Nuvolari. In the 1935 German Grand Prix, Nuvolari drove the old-fashioned Alfa P3 to a staggering victory over a field of cutting-edge Mercedes and Auto-Unions, to the bewilderment of the officiating Nazis. He performed similar miracles with Alfa on several occasions in 1936.

Following the death of Auto Union's Bernd Rosemeyer, and the ill-health of Varzi, Nuvolari was recruited by Auto Union part-way through 1938. Despite never having raced mid-engined machines before, he showed that, at the age of 45, his genius was still intact. He took two victories, including a stirring comeback drive in that year's Donington Grand Prix and the 1939 Czechoslovakian Grand Prix.

Post-war, Nuvolari took up the sport once more but by now he was an ill man, and he frequently had to retire from races coughing up blood. Still he couldn't stop, and still the miraculous performances unfolded. In both the 1947 and 1948 Mille Miglia races, he was robbed of victory after truly staggering drives. He died in 1953.

◀ **Nuvolari driving for Auto Union in 1938.**

Riccardo Patrese

Patrese is the holder of the record for the greatest number of Grand Prix starts. Between 1977 and 1993 the Italian lined up to do battle on the Formula One grid no less than 256 times. He won on six occasions for the Brabham and Williams teams.

A graduate of karting, he rose to car racing prominence in Formula Three and Formula Two, and made his Formula One debut with the Shadow team at Monaco in 1977. A new team, Arrows, was formed for 1978 from Shadow, and Patrese became their lead driver. In only the team's second race, Patrese was dominating the South African Grand Prix when the car failed. He was the only driver in the team's history to have put an Arrows on pole position – a feat he achieved at Long Beach, in the United States in 1981.

Patrese's first victory didn't come until he transferred to Brabham, for whom he won the 1982 Monaco Grand Prix. After an interlude at Alfa Romeo he stayed with Brabham until Bernie Ecclestone sold it at the end of 1987. Patrese transferred to Williams in 1988, and went on to win four races for the team between 1990 and 1992. After a season with Benetton alongside Michael Schumacher in 1993, Patrese brought his distinguished career to an end.

Riccardo Patrese	
Nationality	Italian
Seasons	1977–93
Teams driven for	Shadow, Arrows, Brabham, Williams, Alfa Romeo, Benetton
Number of major victories	6

◀ Riccardo Patrese in 1988.

▼ (*below*) Patrese in his first Formula One season, finishing sixth for Shadow at the Japanese Grand Prix at Fuji in 1977.

▼ (*bottom*) Patrese in 1993, his final season in Formula One, driving for Benetton at the South African Grand Prix.

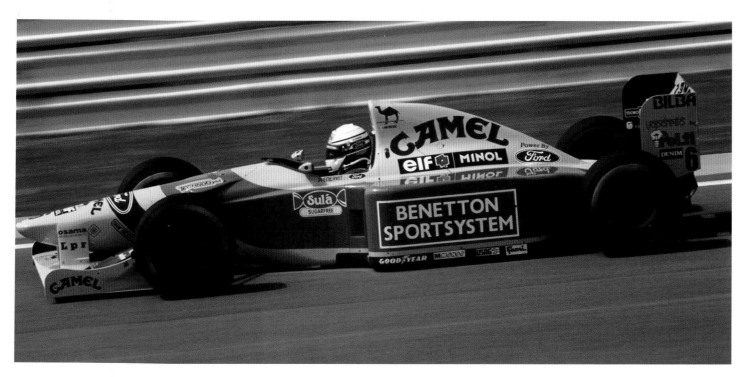

Ronnie Peterson

The Swede was known unofficially as "the world's fastest driver" during the peak of his career in the 1970s. Although he never managed to translate this tag into the World Championship title, he was twice runner-up and lit up many races with some electrifying performances and astonishing car control.

Winning the 1969 Monaco Formula Three race proved to be his catapult into Formula One the following year. In 1971, driving for March, he finished runner-up to Jackie Stewart in the World Championship. But it wasn't until his move to Lotus in 1973 that he began winning races. In 1973, he set what was then a record of nine pole positions during the season, and his raw speed comfortably eclipsed that of his reigning World Champion team-mate, Emerson Fittipaldi.

Lotus cars subsequently lost their competitiveness and Peterson left for a couple of barren seasons of his own, before returning in 1978, this time as a contracted number two driver to the incumbent Mario Andretti. Lotus were by now the dominant team once again,

▲ Ronnie Peterson in his Lotus 72E on his way to second place in the British Grand Prix at Silverstone in 1973, the year in which he set nine pole positions.

Ronnie Peterson

Nationality	Swedish
Seasons	1970–78
Teams driven for	Lotus, March, Tyrrell
Number of major victories	10

thanks to their 79 model. Although there were several races where Peterson was quicker than his team-mate, he dutifully fulfilled his contracted role. Two wins, including a superb wet weather performance in Austria, confirmed his speed was very much still there. At the Italian Grand Prix, he was involved in a startline collision, and his car was thrown into the barriers, breaking one of his legs. That night he died from a brain embolism triggered by the broken bone. His second place in the Championship to Andretti was thus taken posthumously.

▲ Ronnie Peterson in 1971. He died following an accident at the start of the Italian Grand Prix in 1978.

◄ Peterson finished a close second in the 1971 Italian Grand Prix after leading for much of the race.

Nelson Piquet

▼ Piquet's Brabham BT49C took third place at Long Beach in 1981, the scene of his first victory 12 months earlier.

The great Brazilian driver won three World Championships in the 1980s, and brought his long Formula One career to a close at the end of 1991, a season during which he proved he was still capable of winning races.

The son of a diplomat, Piquet moved to Europe to pursue the career he had begun in his homeland, inspired by the success of Emerson Fittipaldi. He was recruited by the Brabham team at the end of 1978, after winning that year's British Formula Three Championship and making a few Formula One appearances with a privately-run McLaren. Teamed alongside Niki Lauda at Brabham in 1979 he proved every bit as quick, and following Lauda's retirement, Piquet entered 1980 as the clear team leader. After winning his first Grand Prix at Long Beach, he

Nelson Piquet

Nationality	Brazilian
Seasons	1978–91
Teams driven for	Ensign, Brabham, Williams, Lotus, Benetton
Number of major victories	23

▼ Nelson Piquet, three times World Champion, seen here in 1986.

challenged Williams' Alan Jones hard for the title, but ultimately had to wait until 1981 for his first Championship.

He repeated the feat two years later, in the turbocharged Brabham-BMW, after a dramatic late-season comeback to overhaul a big points deficit to rival Alain Prost. The Brabham team's form dwindled subsequently, and Piquet switched to Williams for 1986, only narrowly losing out on the title. He won it in 1987 despite a big shunt at Imola that dulled his speed for some time afterwards. After poor seasons with

Lotus in 1988–89, many believed he was a spent force when Benetton recruited him in 1990. But he proved the doubters wrong with victories in the final two races of the year. He won again in Canada 1991 but retired from Formula One at the end of the season. He subsequently incurred serious leg injuries while practising for the 1992 Indianapolis 500.

▼ Piquet took a great victory in the 1987 Hungarian Grand Prix after passing the Lotus of Ayrton Senna.

Didier Pironi

Frenchman Pironi looked to be on his way to the 1982 World Championship when he suffered a career-ending accident during the warm-up session for the German Grand Prix at Hockenheim.

The son of a wealthy construction company boss, he rose through the Elf-sponsored ranks of French junior racing in the 1970s, before graduating to Formula Two in 1977. There, he finished third in the Championship but earned wider recognition when he stepped back down to Formula Three for a one-off race supporting the 1977 Monaco Grand Prix, and won it. This was the springboard for his Formula One debut with Tyrrell in 1978.

It was not until he joined the more competitive Ligier team in 1980 that Pironi really began to show what he could do. He took his first Grand Prix victory in Belgium and produced some stunningly fast drives, not all of which were rewarded, through no fault of his own. His form in the Ligier led to his recruitment to Ferrari for the following year. Paired alongside Gilles Villeneuve, he struggled initially but with a much improved car for 1982 he began to look strong once more.

He took victory in the San Marino Grand Prix in controversial circumstances, Villeneuve feeling that Pironi had duped

Didier Pironi	
Nationality	French
Seasons	1978–82
Teams driven for	Tyrrell, Ligier, Ferrari
Number of major victories	3

◄ **Didier Pironi celebrates his third victory at the Dutch Grand Prix in 1982. This result put him in the lead for that year's World Championship title.**

▼ **Pironi took his Ligier JS11/15 to his maiden victory at the Belgian Grand Prix at Spa in 1980.**

him and gone against team orders in passing him on the last lap. After Villeneuve's subsequent fatal accident, Pironi assumed leadership of the team. He won again in Holland, and by the time of the German Grand Prix had a comfortable Championship lead.

He crashed in conditions of blinding spray, hitting the back of Alain Prost's Renault at very high speed. The Ferrari reared high in the air before crashing down, and Pironi suffered serious leg injuries. Though he recovered, his right foot was no longer strong enough for the heavy braking required and he quietly retired. He took up power boating, and was killed competing in a race off the Isle of Wight in 1987.

◄ **Pironi in the Ferrari 126C2, the fastest car of 1982.**

Alain Prost

Winner of four World Championships and 51 Grands Prix, Frenchman Prost is statistically the second most successful driver in the sport's history, behind Michael Schumacher.

His Formula One career spanned 13 years, during which time he earned a reputation for searing speed disguised beneath silky smoothness. One of the most analytical of drivers, he was nicknamed The Professor.

He made his Formula One debut with McLaren in 1980 after winning the 1979 European Formula Three Championship. Promising form there led to his recruitment by Renault, for whom he won his first Grand Prix in 1981. Tension with team-mate René Arnoux in 1982 led to Prost's clear status as team leader in 1983. He established a big lead early in the Championship that year, but was ultimately thwarted by the late-season pace of Nelson Piquet's Brabham-BMW. He was sensationally sacked by Renault in the aftermath of losing the title, but this worked to his advantage in that he was able to sign for McLaren the following season, and McLaren produced the fastest car of 1984. Prost became locked in battle for the title with his team-mate Niki Lauda, but lost out by half a point in the last round.

But Prost couldn't be denied forever. He took a comfortable championship victory with McLaren in 1985, a feat he repeated in 1986, becoming the first back-to-back title winner since Jack Brabham in 1959–60. He was joined at McLaren in 1988 by Ayrton Senna, and so began one of the most dramatic and long-running feuds in Formula One. He lost out to his team-mate in the 1988 title battle, but won in 1989 after controversially blocking Senna's passing move in Japan. Transferring to Ferrari for 1990, he again battled with Senna's McLaren for the title, this time coming off second when Senna drove into him – again in Japan.

He was sacked from Ferrari after a disappointing 1991 season and sat out the following year. He returned in 1993

▲ Alain Prost, World Drivers' Champion in 1985, 1986, 1989 and 1993.

Alain Prost	
Nationality	French
Seasons	1980–93
Teams driven for	McLaren, Renault, Ferrari, Williams
Number of major victories	51

with Williams, and took his fourth title in the best car in the field. He retired – as the most successful driver in the sport's history – and turned team owner in 1997, after buying Ligier and renaming it Prost. The team went into receivership at the end of 2001.

► Prost won at Monaco in 1984, but was awarded only half points. It cost him the title.

Kimi Raikkonen

Raikkonen took over very big shoes when he stepped in to replace fellow Finn Mika Häkkinen at McLaren at the end of 2001.

Raikkonen was just 21 years old when, in 2001, he made his Grand Prix debut with Sauber. This marked only his second season of car racing. After a successful karting career he had graduated to cars in 2000, winning the British Formula Renault Championship. Inexperience proved to be little handicap in Formula One as he scored several World Championship points and was often quicker than his more experienced team-mate Nick Heidfeld.

Such performances brought Raikkonen to the attention of the McLaren team, where in 2002 he produced several stunning performances. He was within a few laps of winning the French Grand Prix that year when a backmarker's oil spillage cost him dearly. He won the 2003 Malaysian Grand Prix and followed it up with a campaign that took him to the final round with a chance of the World Championship. In the end he had to settle for runner-up to Michael Schumacher, but few would bet against him going one better in the future.

Kimi Raikkonen

Nationality	Finnish
Seasons	2001–present
Teams driven for	Sauber, McLaren
Number of major victories	1

◀ Kimi Raikkonen in 2002.

▼ (below) In the Sauber-Petronas C20 at the Australian Grand Prix, Melbourne, 2001.

▼ (bottom) In 2003, Raikkonen took victory in Malaysia and scored consistently high places throughout the season.

Marcel Renault

Marcel backed his elder brother Louis in establishing the Renault company at the turn of the 20th century, and together they raced the cars that Louis's factory built. Although both proved to be among the leading drivers of the day, it was Marcel who was particularly brilliant.

With Louis he had owned a repair shop in Billancourt for a steam yacht they both owned. His engineering skills then helped Louis develop an improved gearbox on Louis's de Dion car. When they went into business to produce cars, Marcel helped his brother fund it all. With a voiturette car that was far less powerful than the opposition, Marcel won the 1902 Paris–Vienna race outright. He was charging through the field in the 1903 Paris–Madrid when he tangled with Leon Théry. The Renault

Marcel Renault	
Nationality	French
Seasons	1900–03
Teams driven for	Renault
Number of major victories	1

speared off into a tree and Marcel received injuries from which he later died. His brother Louis – who finished the race second, not knowing of Marcel's accident – retired from race driving with immediate effect.

◀ **Marcel Renault in 1903.**

▼ **Marcel Renault competing in the 1903 Paris–Madrid race in his Renault.**

Carlos Reutemann

he Argentinian driver proved
an often inspired performer in
a Formula One career that lasted from
1972 to 1982, but losing the 1981
Championship to Nelson Piquet in the
final round proved to be as close as
he ever got to the world crown.

One of only three men to set pole
position on their Grand Prix debuts,
Reutemann achieved this feat at the
1972 Argentine Grand Prix, driving for
Brabham. It was the beginning of a
long love affair for the home fans, and
Reutemann was a national hero for
the rest of his career.

He took his first Grand Prix victories
with the Brabham BT44 of 1974 and
1975 . His performances were occasionally
in a class of their own, reducing
everyone else to mere support roles, but
finding such a level consistently proved
to be elusive. Recruited to Ferrari at the
end of 1976, he won races for them in
1977 and 1978, finishing third in the
Championship in the latter year. A move
to Lotus in 1979 proved ill-timed and
he moved onto Williams for 1980,
winning the Monaco Grand Prix and
again finishing third in the title chase.

He began 1981 at the peak of his
powers and after disobeying team
orders to beat Alan Jones in Brazil,

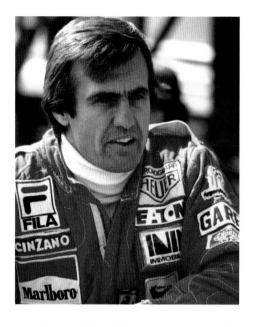

Carlos Reutemann	
Nationality	Argentinian
Seasons	1972–82
Teams driven for	Brabham, Ferrari, Lotus, Williams
Number of major victories	12

◀ **Carlos Reutemann, an enigmatic performer for 10 years. On his day he was unbeatable.**

▼ **Reutemann won from pole at the USA Grand Prix in 1974 in his Brabham BT44, the third victory of his season.**

he went on to lead the Championship
by a handsome margin by mid-season.
The second half of his year was
disappointing and, as Piquet caught up
his points tally, they entered the final
round in Las Vegas separated by just
one point. Despite scoring a brilliant
pole position, Reutemann had a
disappointing race and finished eighth.
With Piquet finishing fifth, Reutemann
lost the Championship. He announced
his retirement but changed his mind
before the beginning of the 1982 season.
He took second place in the South
African Grand Prix, but after one more
race decided that he did want to retire
after all, and turned his back on the
sport. He has since established himself
as a leading politician in Argentina.

◀ **Reutemann took a great second place in his non-turbo Williams at the 1982 South African Grand Prix, his penultimate race.**

Jochen Rindt

Austrian Jochen Rindt became 1970 World Champion posthumously. He was killed at Monza that season, practising for the Italian Grand Prix. But in the remaining four races no-one was able to overhaul the points score he had built up from five victories earlier in the year.

He funded his early racing by selling the business inherited from parents who were killed in a wartime air-raid. He broke onto the international scene when, as a virtual unknown, he beat Graham Hill to win a Formula Two race at Crystal Palace in 1964. He made his Formula One debut later that year, at his home race with Rob Walker. For the next three years, he drove Cooper's outdated cars, finishing third in the 1966 Championship. A move to Brabham in 1968 underlined his stunning turn of speed, but the cars were unreliable. This led to him taking up an offer to join Lotus for 1969. In Colin Chapman's 49 model, he was devastatingly fast but didn't win until the final race of the year, in the USA.

For 1970, Lotus produced the ground-breaking 72 model. Initially it proved uncompetitive and Rindt gave the old 49 an unbelievable last-lap victory at Monaco. Thereafter, he transferred to the 72 and rattled off four consecutive wins. He had confided to friends that if he won the 1970 title, he would consider retirement. It was an option he was never granted.

▲ Jochen Rindt on his way to victory at the Dutch Grand Prix of 1970. It was one of five wins that season.

Jochen Rindt	
Nationality	Austrian
Seasons	1964–70
Teams driven for	Cooper, Brabham, Lotus
Number of major victories	6

◄ Rindt only hours before his death at the Italian Grand Prix, Monza, September 1970. He was said to be contemplating retirement.

▲ Rindt's Lotus 72 runs without wings. It was perhaps a contributory factor in his fatal accident at Monza, which occured a short while after this picture was taken.

▶ Rindt's Brabham BT24 – here at South Africa – was fast but unreliable in 1968.

Pedro Rodriguez

▼ Pedro Rodriguez had to settle for second place, at the Dutch Grand Prix at Zandvoort in 1971, after suffering a misfire.

The Mexican Rodriguez was often a spectacular performer in Formula One from the late 1960s until his death in a sports car accident in 1971.

The elder brother of Ferrari driver Ricardo Rodriguez, the pair had caused a sensation in sports car racing in the late 1950s when, as teenagers, they enjoyed success at an international level, funded initially by their wealthy businessman father. When Ricardo was killed practising for the 1962 Mexican Grand Prix, Pedro considered retirement, but returned for more sports car success. He made occasional Formula One appearances, notably with Lotus and Ferrari, but these never led to permanent seats. For the 1967 South African Grand Prix he was offered a drive by Cooper – and he went on to win the race, thus securing his drive for the rest of the season.

At BRM in 1968 he frequently showed great speed, particularly in the wet. He also won the Le Mans 24 Hours sports car race that year for Ford, partnered by Lucien Bianchi. BRM gave him a competitive but unreliable car in 1970, and he won the Belgian Grand Prix with it. In the wet 1971 Dutch Grand Prix, he fought for the lead with fellow wet-weather maestro Jacky Ickx, but finished second after the car developed a misfire. His sports car drives for Porsche during this time were quite sensational, and he was undoubtedly one of the world's greatest drivers when he crashed to his death in a minor sports car race at the Norisring in Germany in July 1971. Deeply fatalistic he had always said that God chooses when it's your time.

Pedro Rodriguez	
Nationality	Mexican
Seasons	1963–71
Teams driven for	Lotus, Ferrari, Cooper, BRM
Number of major victories	2

▼ Pedro Rodriguez at the British Grand Prix, Brands Hatch, in 1970,

◄ Rodriguez was enjoying his strongest season in 1971, with the BRM P160 in Formula One, and with Porsche in sportscar.

Keke Rosberg

The World Champion of 1982, Rosberg was the first Finn to be successful in Formula One, blazing a path that others have since followed.

A tough, shrewd operator, he made his way up the racing ladder through enterprise, hard graft and a lot of talent. But even so, it was a struggle and by the time he made it to Formula One in 1978 he was already 29. In the non-championship International Trophy – his third ever Formula One race – he took the unfancied Theodore car to victory. But even this did not attract him to the top teams, and he served his time with ATS and Fittipaldi.

It was the late-notice retirement of Alan Jones at the end of 1981 that created Rosberg's opportunity with Williams. He responded by winning his first Grand Prix at Dijon 1982 and scoring highly throughout the season to clinch the Championship in the final round. He won a handful of races in his remaining three years with Williams, but he was never a Championship contender. He drove for McLaren in his final season of 1986 and was leading his final race, in Australia, when his car suddenly stopped.

His subsequent activities included racing in touring and sports car, managing the career of Mika Häkkinen and latterly that of son, Niko Rosberg.

Keke Rosberg	
Nationality	Finnish
Seasons	1978–86
Teams driven for	Theodore, ATS, Wolf, Fittipaldi, Williams, McLaren
Number of major victories	5

▲ Rosberg in his McLaren MP4/2C during his final Grand Prix, at Adelaide in 1986. He was leading the race when the car failed.

▼ (left) Rosberg cut a colourful figure in Formula One during the 1980s, and a cigarette was rarely far from his lips.

▼ (right) Rosberg took victory with Theodore in the International Trophy race at Silverstone in 1978.

Bernd Rosemeyer

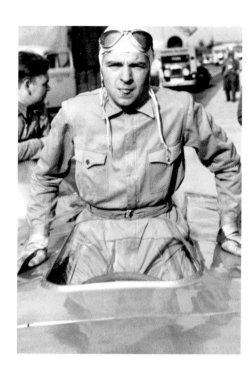

osemeyer burst onto the Grand Prix scene of the mid-1930s like a meteorite, instantly causing a sensation with his speed for Auto Union, this despite never having raced a car of any description before, his only racing experience being with motorcycles.

The DKW team for which he raced motorcycles was part of the Auto Union group, and he got a trial in the awesome V16, mid-engined machine at the end of 1934, and subsequently made his debut part-way through 1935. He was heading for victory in his second-ever race before a misfire held him back to second. In his first full season of 1936, he became European Champion. His drives left onlookers spellbound, his talent seemingly limitless. He was widely considered to be the world's fastest driver during his brief career.

Bernd Rosemeyer	
Nationality	German
Seasons	1935–37
Teams driven for	Auto Union
Number of major victories	5

It all came to an end in January 1938. Attempting to set a world speed record for Auto Union on a German autobahn, a side wind blew his car out of control at over 400km/h (250mph). He was killed after hitting some trees.

◀ Bernd Rosemeyer.

▼ Rosemeyer in the Auto Union C type at the Donington Grand Prix in 1937.

Jody Scheckter

The 1979 World Champion for Ferrari, South African Scheckter, entered Formula One in the early 1970s with a "wild boy" tag, and he left it as a respected elder statesman at the end of 1980.

After winning a "Driver to Europe" scheme in South Africa, Scheckter made his name in British Formula Ford and Formula Three racing. He was picked up by McLaren to drive its Formula Two car and by the end of that season, 1972, he was making his Grand Prix debut for the team.

He was comfortably leading the 1973 French Grand Prix, only his third Formula One race, until hit by Emerson Fittipaldi. In the following race at Silverstone, he created an impact for the wrong reasons, when his spin into the pit wall on the first lap took out much of the field. Despite this, he was chosen by Ken Tyrrell as the lead driver of his team in 1974, in the wake of Jackie Stewart's retirement and the

▼ Jody Scheckter's Wolf WR1 leads John Watson's Brabham at the Monaco Grand Prix of 1977. Scheckter won.

Jody Scheckter	
Nationality	South African
Seasons	1972–80
Teams driven for	McLaren, Tyrrell, Wolf, Ferrari
Number of major victories	10

death of François Cevert. He justified his selection with a strong third place in the World Championship, winning two Grands Prix along the way. In 1976, he became the only man to win a Grand Prix in a car with other than four wheels, when he took the six-wheel Tyrrell P34 to victory in Sweden. A move to the new Wolf team for 1977 saw Scheckter perform brilliantly, winning

on the team's debut in Argentina and leading the World Championship until mid-season. But it was his move to Ferrari for 1979 that consolidated his status. Three victories and some mature performances clinched him the title comfortably, with two rounds to go.

▼ Jody Scheckter led the 1973 French Grand Prix in this McLaren.

▲ Scheckter in 1980, the year of his retirement from Formula One.

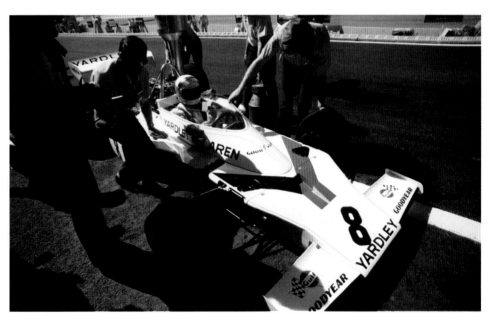

Michael Schumacher

The most successful driver of all time, six-time champion Schumacher continues to rack up success upon success after over a decade in Formula One.

With his early career subsidized by Mercedes-Benz, he graduated from German Formula Three into the World Sportscar Championship with the Mercedes team. His speed there created a sensation and marked him out as a likely Formula One star. His Grand Prix chance came with Jordan at the 1991 Belgian Grand Prix, where he was quicker than team-mate Andrea de Cesaris. By the next race he had been snapped up by Benetton, and he proceeded to outpace triple World Champion Nelson Piquet.

He won his first Grand Prix at Spa in 1992, the first anniversary of his debut. By 1994, he was ready to push for the Championship and was engaged in battle with his biggest rival, Ayrton Senna, when the Brazilian crashed to his death at Imola. In a controversial duel with the Williams of title rival Damon Hill at the final round in Australia, Schumacher drove his damaged car into Hill's, forcing them both to retire but ensuring the title was Michael's. He repeated the feat in 1995, this time without controversy.

◄ Schumacher caused a sensation by qualifying a Jordan in seventh place on his Formula One debut at Spa in 1991.

▼ (below left) Michael Schumacher, took his fifth world title in 2002.

Michael Schumacher

Nationality	German
Seasons	1991–present
Teams driven for	Jordan, Benetton, Ferrari
Number of major victories	70

He then took up the challenge of turning the troubled Ferrari team back into world beaters. He had a difficult first season with them in 1996 but, aided subsequently by the arrival of his design team from Benetton, Ross Brawn and Rory Byrne, he piloted an ever-faster succession of Ferraris. He lost the 1997 title fight to Jacques Villeneuve, when a similar move to the one he'd pulled on Hill went wrong, leaving him in the gravel trap, with Villeneuve continuing. He again lost out in the last round in 1998, this time to Mika Häkkinen. In 1999, he broke his leg at Silverstone, leaving him out for much of the season.

But in 2000 came the crowning glory of his career, when he won the title, the first Ferrari driver to do so for 21 years. He was a dominant champion in 2001, passing Alain Prost's record of 51 Grand Prix victories along the way, and even more successful in 2002, winning a record 11 races in that season alone. This brought him level with the record held since 1957 by Juan Manuel Fangio, and in 2003 he went on to beat that watermark by clinching championship number six at the final round in Japan.

◄ The Ferrari team celebrate Schumacher's Canadian Grand Prix victory in 2003.

Ralf Schumacher

▼ Ralf Schumacher guides his Williams-BMW FW23 to his first Formula One victory at Imola in 2001.

T he younger brother of Michael Schumacher is a highly talented Formula One racer in his own right, and has taken a succession of victories with the Williams-BMW team.

After a karting career, Ralf took up junior car racing in his native Germany, progressing to the German Formula Three Championship in 1995, where he was runner-up. A move to the Japanese Formula Nippon series in 1996 secured him a major championship, and this proved his springboard to Formula One with the Jordan team in 1997.

He was extremely quick from the start, but initially rather accident-prone. This continued until half-way through

◄ (far left) Ralf Schumacher has driven for Williams since 1999.

◄ (left) Ralf was immediately quick in his debut season of 1997 with Jordan.

the 1998 season, after which his performances became notably more mature. He was catching team-mate Damon Hill in the Belgian Grand Prix and looked ready to take the victory, before team orders were imposed, leaving him a frustrated second.

He moved to Williams in 1999, a team that initially couldn't offer him a

Ralf Schumacher

Nationality	German
Seasons	1997–present
Teams driven for	Jordan, Williams
Number of major victories	6

potentially race-winning car but which promised a future partnership with BMW. This came good in 2001, with Ralf taking his first victory at Imola and following it with two more. He continued his race-winning form into 2002 and 2003, and in due course he could well become the second member of the Schumacher family to win a world title.

▼ Ralf Schumacher took his Jordan-Peugeot to third place in the Argentinian Grand Prix in 1997.

Henry Segrave

egrave was the first British driver to win a Grand Prix when he took his Sunbeam to victory in France in 1923. In his short time in top flight racing, before he took up the challenge of the landspeed record, he established himself among the elite of drivers.

A British national, he was born in Baltimore in the United States, but raised in Ireland and educated at Eton, England. After serving in World War I, his imagination was captured by motorsport when he spectated at an American race. He took up the sport at Brooklands in Britain, and badgered Sunbeam racing boss Louis Coatalen to be included in Sunbeam's works team in 1921. In the 1922 French Grand Prix, he ran as high as third before retiring, assuring himself a permanent place on the Sunbeam team. Following his victory of 1923, he was dominating the early stages of the 1924 race when the Sunbeam's electrics played up. He took some consolation with victory in the San Sebastian Grand Prix, in Spain, later in the year. After a further win at Miramas, France in 1926, he retired from racing altogether to concentrate on speed records.

In 1927, he became the first man to exceed 322km/h (200mph) and in 1929, he raised the record to 372.46km/h (231.44mph) in the Irving-Napier Golden Arrow. Later that year, he was killed attempting a water speed record, when his boat hit a log on Lake Windermere. He was 34.

▲ *(left)* Henry Segrave.

◄ Segrave in his Sunbeam at the French Grand Prix at Tours in 1923. He won the race.

▼ The 1921 Grand Prix at Le Mans. Segrave (10) finished ninth, and Jimmy Murphy in the Deusenberg (12) was the winner.

Henry Segrave	
Nationality	British
Seasons	1921–26
Teams driven for	Sunbeam
Number of major victories	3

Ayrton Senna

The World Champion of 1988, 1990 and 1991, Brazilian Senna proved himself one of the greatest exponents of the sport ever seen until his death at the 1994 San Marino Grand Prix.

He came to Britain to make his name after a successful karting career in Brazil that began when he was a child. He dominated in British Formula Ford, Formula 2000 and Formula Three, leading to Formula One tests with Williams, Brabham and McLaren in 1983. He opted, though, to make his debut with the smaller Toleman team for 1984. At a wet Monaco, in only his fifth Grand Prix, he was closing down fast on leader Alain Prost and looked set to pass when the race was stopped short of its allocated distance. Such form led to his recruitment by Lotus for 1985. He took his first victory at Estoril in Portugal, with an astonishing display of virtuosity in the wet conditions.

Further wins followed with Lotus, but it was no longer a World Championship calibre team, and for 1988 he joined McLaren – alongside the great Prost. It was arguably the strongest driver line up of all time and it was inevitable that their relationship became difficult. Amid some incredibly intense battles, Senna emerged on top in 1988, Prost in 1989. Senna's clinching of the 1990 title by aiming his car at Prost's Ferrari and not lifting as they reached the first corner added to the impression that utter ruthlessness backed up his talent. Although the 1992 and 1993 McLarens were outclassed by the cars of Williams, Senna still produced some stunning drives, none more so than at Donington, England, in 1993, when, in wet conditions, he put in one of his greatest ever performances to win.

He transferred to Williams for 1994, setting pole position for the first three races, taking his tally to 65, still an all-time record. He was leading at Imola from his new rival, Michael Schumacher, when he crashed to his death. Motorsport – and the nation of Brazil – went into deep mourning.

▶ Senna caused a sensation by taking a Toleman to second place at the rain-soaked Monaco Grand Prix in 1984.

▲ Ayrton Senna tragically lost his life in an accident on lap six of the San Marino Grand Prix at Imola, 1 May 1994.

◀ Senna at the Mexican Grand Prix, Mexico City, in 1992.

Ayrton Senna	
Nationality	Brazilian
Seasons	1984–94
Teams driven for	Toleman, Lotus, McLaren, Williams
Number of major victories	41

Raymond Sommer

This French driver was responsible for some of the greatest giant-killing acts seen in Grand Prix racing, from his early years in the 1930s up to the time of his death in 1950.

The son of a pioneer aviator, he was from a sufficiently wealthy background that he was able to indulge his passion for speed. He bought a succession of ex-works Grand Prix cars from Alfa Romeo and Maserati, and prepared and entered them himself. His form frequently embarrassed the works teams with the latest equipment, and he was repeatedly offered factory drives, but invariably turned them down. Fiercely independent, he preferred to race on his own terms.

In the 1932 Marseilles Grand Prix, Sommer sensationally defeated the factory Alfa and Maserati teams with his old Alfa Monza. It was a performance he looked on-course to repeat at Spa in 1950 when, at 43 years of age and with an outclassed Talbot, he pushed the far faster Alfa Romeos. Initially the Alfa pit crew believed he couldn't possibly be on the same lap, but he was. It was to Alfa's great relief

▲ **Raymond Sommer racing a Maserati in Jersey in 1947.**

that the Talbot broke down and took him out of the race, but those with long memories weren't surprised.

Sommer was killed competing in a minor French hillclimb event at the end of the year, when it is believed a wheelbearing on his Cooper seized.

Raymond Sommer	
Nationality	French
Seasons	1932–50
Teams driven for	Alfa Romeo, Ferrari
Number of major victories	3

▲ **Sommer at the Italian Grand Prix in 1950.**

◄ **Sommer's Alfa Romeo finished second at the 1946 Nice Grand Prix. Here he is leading Chaboud in the Delahaye.**

Jackie Stewart

Triple World Champion Jackie Stewart is remembered not only for his masterly performances behind the wheel, but also for initiating and progressing the sport's safety campaign in the late 1960s up to his retirement from racing in 1973.

The Scot began his single-seater career in British Formula Three, where he was a dominant champion in 1964, driving for Ken Tyrrell's team. He moved straight into Formula One in 1965 with BRM, scoring his first Grand Prix win that year and ending up third in the World Championship.

It was an incredible rookie year, but success was harder to come by in the two seasons that followed. In 1966 he suffered a frightening accident in the Belgian Grand Prix and it was this that initiated his safety campaign, something that continued throughout and beyond his driving career.

For 1968, he hooked up once more with Tyrrell who ran a Matra-Ford for him and the winning ways returned. He only narrowly missed out on that year's Championship, and in 1969 the partnership was dominant as Stewart took his first world title.

With the new "Tyrrell" car Stewart dominated in 1971, but a stomach ulcer compromised his 1972 season. He began 1973 having decided he would retire at the end of the year, though this was a secret shared by only his inner circle. He won five Grands Prix that year, and clinched his third title with a stunning recovery drive at Monza that showed he was every bit as fast as he'd ever been.

He subsequently continued his long relationship with Ford, and in 1996 became a Formula One team owner as he established Stewart Grand Prix, with Ford backing. The team won the 1999 European Grand Prix with Johnny Herbert, but Ford subsequently bought out Stewart and rebranded the team as Jaguar.

▲ Jackie Stewart was restricted to fifth place in the USA Grand Prix in 1971 because of chunking tyres on his Tyrrell 003.

◄ Stewart in 1971, the year of his second World Drivers' Championship title. This was his first season in the new Tyrrell car.

Jackie Stewart

Nationality	British
Seasons	1965–73
Teams driven for	BRM, Tyrrell
Number of major victories	27

► Stewart outran BRM team-mate Graham Hill to win his first Grand Prix in his debut year, at Italy in 1965.

John Surtees

This Englishman is the only person to have won World Championships in both motorcycle racing and Formula One. He was one of the greatest drivers of the 1960s, and could conceivably have been even more successful had he made different career choices.

Between 1956 and 1960, Surtees won seven world titles in various motorcycle classes. He made his Grand Prix debut with Lotus in 1960, and his enormous potential on four wheels was made clear when he scored pole position at Portugal in only his third Grand Prix.

After two seasons in privateer teams, he was recruited by Ferrari for 1963. He won in Germany that year, and his analytical approach was fundamental in improving the team's competitiveness. This progressed into 1964 when, after a particularly strong second half of the season, he clinched the Championship at the final round. At the end of 1965, he suffered a serious accident in a Can-Am sports car, in which he was lucky to survive.

Impressively, he recovered in time for the start of the 1966 season. He and Ferrari were favourites for the title, and he took a superb victory in the wet

▲ Pole sitter John Surtees retired on lap 36 of the 1960 Portuguese Grand Prix.

John Surtees

Nationality	British
Seasons	1960–72
Teams driven for	Lotus, Ferrari, Cooper, Honda, BRM, Surtees
Number of major victories	6

Belgian Grand Prix. Following a row with the Ferrari team manager, he left and drove the rest of the season for Cooper, winning the Mexican Grand Prix.

Thereafter, he was involved with the Honda Formula One project – giving the team victory in the 1967 Italian Grand Prix – and with BRM, before going off to form his own Formula One team. His last full season in the driving seat was 1971, after which he concentrated on running the team. In eight years of toil, Team Surtees was never able to succeed in the same way as Surtees the driver.

▲ John Surtees in 1968.

◄ Surtees in the Honda RA300 (car 14) leads Chris Amon's Ferrari 312 at the Italian Grand Prix, Monza, in 1967.

Leon Théry

Recognized as the greatest driver of his era, Théry won the Gordon Bennett Cup races – the equivalent of a World Championship today – in 1904 and 1905, driving Richard-Brasier cars.

Known as "The Chronometer" for his incredibly consistent speed, he won in machinery that was no better than that of his leading rivals, who would invariably make mistakes as they tried in vain to keep up. He was also noted for his very thorough preparation, and would spend weeks testing his cars before the races.

He left Richard-Brasier along with co-founder Georges Richard in 1906, to set up a new car company, though this was unsuccessful. He returned to Brasier for the 1908 French Grand Prix and ran third until the car failed. He died a year later from tuberculosis.

▲ A portrait of Leon Théry in 1904 after winning the Gordon Bennett cup.

▶ Théry in the 1905 Gordon Bennett trophy race in a Brasier. He won this race just as he had won the 1904 event.

Leon Théry	
Nationality	French
Seasons	1903–08
Teams driven for	Richard-Braiser
Number of major victories	4

Wolfgang von Trips

▼ Wolfgang von Trips during the 1960 Argentine Grand Prix in his Ferrari.

he German count was leading the World Championship for Ferrari, in 1961, when he crashed to his death during the Italian Grand Prix at Monza.

After beginning his career in sports car racing in the 1950s, von Trips was taken on by Ferrari, driving his first Grand Prix for the team at Monza in 1956. He was retained as an occasional driver by the team for the next three years, but got his chance as a full-time member in 1960 after the departures of Tony Brooks and Dan Gurney.

In between racing that season, he conducted much development work on the new mid-engined Ferrari, and this put him in good stead for the 1961

Wolfgang von Trips	
Nationality	German
Seasons	1956–61
Teams driven for	Ferrari
Number of major victories	2

season, when the 156 "sharknose" model was the fastest car in the field. He battled with his team-mate Phil Hill for the destiny of the crown, winning both the Dutch and British Grand Prix, and had a narrow points lead over the American as they began the penultimate round of the championship at Monza.

After a poor start, he was making his way towards the front. On lap three, he passed Jim Clark, but Clark's Lotus then slipstreamed him down the

following straight, and under braking for the Parabolica turn, moved to von Trips' inside to repass. Probably not realizing the Lotus was still there, von Trips moved the same way as Clark. Their wheels interlocked and the Ferrari was thrown up the banking and along the fence, killing 14 spectators along the way. Von Trips was thrown out on to the track, and killed upon impact. Germany would have to wait another 33 years for its first World Champion.

▲ Wolfgang von Trips after winning the 1961 British Grand Prix. It was a brave performance on a rain-soaked track.

◄ Von Trips (Ferrari 156) won the British Grand Prix at Aintree in 1961. He led the World Championship at this point.

Achille Varzi

One of the greatest drivers of the 1930s, Milanese Varzi won Grands Prix for Alfa Romeo, Maserati, Bugatti and Auto Union after a successful career as a motorcycle racer.

Known as "The Ice Man" for his unnatural calm and cool, his clinical but stunningly fast driving reflected his temperament. This formed an elemental contrast with the style of his great adversary, the flamboyant Tazio Nuvolari. The two were rivals in motorcycle racing and moved into car racing together, forming their own team to run a pair of Bugattis.

Although successful, Varzi was uneasy being in the same team as his biggest rival, and moved on to works drives with much success over the years. Many of his victories came after stirring battles with Nuvolari. For 1935, he was recruited by Auto Union and began well, but early in 1936, he became addicted to morphine and his form dropped off alarmingly. He was

▲ Achille Varzi at Monaco in 1933.

Achille Varzi	
Nationality	Italian
Seasons	1928–48
Teams driven for	Alfa Romeo, Maserati, Bugatti, Auto Union
Number of major victories	18

dismissed by the team and did not reappear in racing until after the war, by which time he had kicked the habit and was back in good health.

He immediately began winning races again for Alfa Romeo, but was killed in practice for the 1948 Swiss Grand Prix, when his car overturned as he was attempting to wrest pole position from his team-mate Jean-Pierre Wimille.

▼ Varzi in a Bugatti leads two similar models on the Monaco circuit in 1933.

Gilles Villeneuve

The French-Canadian was one of the fastest, most spectacular drivers the sport has ever seen. He looked set for a glittering future, but was killed after crashing his Ferrari, while qualifying for the Belgian Grand Prix at Zolder in 1982.

Villeneuve started out by racing snowmobiles in Canada, becoming World Champion in the discipline before moving into car racing. A dominant North American Formula Atlantic Champion in 1976, he gained big international recognition when World Champion-elect James Hunt took part in a round of the Atlantic series, as Villeneuve's team-mate, and was beaten by him. Hunt reported back to his Formula One team, McLaren, who entered a third car for Villeneuve in the 1977 British Grand Prix.

His debut in an obsolete model was sensational, and he was set to finish fourth when a faulty temperature gauge sent him to the pits. When Niki Lauda walked out on Ferrari before the season was over, the Italian team recruited Villeneuve as his replacement. At the end of 1978 he won his first Grand Prix – fittingly at his home track of Montreal. For 1979, he was

Gilles Villeneuve	
Nationality	Canadian
Seasons	1977–82
Teams driven for	McLaren, Ferrari
Number of major victories	6

◄ Gilles Villeneuve in 1978, his first full season in Formula One. He took victory in the final race of the season.

▼ Villeneuve made his Grand Prix debut at Silverstone in 1977. He was on course for fourth place. Until a faulty temperature gauge sent him to the pits.

contracted in a support role to the experienced Jody Scheckter, but initially was clearly quicker. He won three Grands Prix that year but stood by team instructions, following Scheckter home at Monza and finishing the season as runner-up in the Championship.

He took two remarkable victories in 1981, with an uncompetitive Ferrari, but began 1982 as title favourite with a much-improved car. He was duped by team-mate Didier Pironi into losing the San Marino Grand Prix and was afterwards furious. Still angry two weeks later in Belgium, he was attempting to beat Pironi's qualifying time when a slower car moved into his path. The Ferrari flew high in the air before crashing down nose-first. Villeneuve was fatally injured.

◄ Villeneuve suffered a very uncompetitive Ferrari in 1980. He finished in fifth place in the Monaco Grand Prix that season.

Jacques Villeneuve

▼ Villeneuve in characteristic hard-charging mode in his BAR 003 at Monza in 2000.

By winning the 1997 World Drivers' Championship, Jacques Villeneuve established himself as a Formula One star in his own right, rather than merely the son of Gilles.

He took up racing in the late 1980s, some years after the death of his father. With no karting experience, he initially struggled in the Italian Formula Three series, but subsequently made quick progress. With sponsorship backing from Players Tobacco, he moved to the United States, won the Formula Atlantic Championship and progressed to Indycars. In 1995, his second season there, he won the Championship as well as the prestigious Indianapolis 500.

This was his springboard to Formula One with the mighty Williams team. In Australia in 1996, he became only the third man to set pole position on his Grand Prix debut. He took his first victory at the Nürburgring a few months later and took the Championship battle

Jacques Villeneuve	
Nationality	Canadian
Seasons	1996–present
Teams driven for	Williams, BAR
Number of major victories	11

with team-mate Damon Hill all the way to the final round, but ultimately finished runner-up.

He clinched the 1997 title at the final round in Jerez, Spain, after his only rival, Ferrari's Michael Schumacher, attempted to drive him off the track. The outcome left Schumacher in the gravel trap and Villeneuve still running.

The Williams team lost its form in 1998, and for 1999 Jacques became part of the new BAR team. In five years of struggle, Villeneuve never came close to winning another race. He and BAR parted company at the end of 2003.

▼ Villeneuve's BAR-Honda 002 comes to a fiery end at the Spanish Grand Prix in 2000.

▲ Jacques Villeneuve has had a tough time, with little success, since winning the World Championship title in 1997.

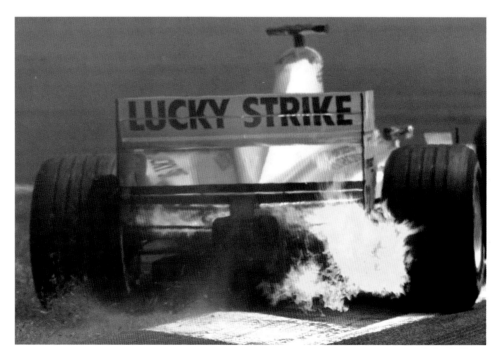

John Watson

The popular Ulsterman was a leading light of Formula One from the mid-1970s to the early 1980s, and only narrowly lost out on the 1982 World Championship.

After a promising but under-funded career in the junior categories, Watson was given his Formula One chance by Bernie Ecclestone's Brabham team in 1973. Unfortunately, he broke his leg on his debut as a result of a sticking throttle. He came back and, in 1974, showed good speed in a privately-entered Brabham. After a half-season in the uncompetitive Surtees for 1975, Watson was recruited by the Penske team at the end of 1975. He gave the team its only Formula One victory with a great drive at Austria in 1976, but even that wasn't enough to prevent the team withdrawing at the season's end.

Back at Brabham for 1977, Watson drove superbly and only appalling luck kept him from winning at least two

John Watson	
Nationality	British
Seasons	1973–84
Teams driven for	Brabham, Surtees, Lotus, Penske, McLaren
Number of major victories	5

◀ **Watson with the beard he wore until he won his first Grand Prix in Austria in 1976.**

Grands Prix. He left at the end of 1978 to join McLaren – unfortunately, just as the team was beginning a downward plunge. It took until 1981 to climb out of the rut, but Watson hung on and took an emotional victory in the British Grand Prix. In 1982, he won at Zolder and Detroit, and took the title battle with Keke Rosberg to the wire in Las

Vegas, but finished second. In his last season in 1983, he took a remarkable victory at Long Beach from 22nd on the grid. He was replaced at McLaren by Alain Prost in 1984.

▼ **John Watson in the Penske PC4 at the Austrian Grand Prix in 1976. It was his first Grand Prix win.**

Jean-Pierre Wimille

At the time of his death, while practising for a race in Argentina in 1949, Wimille was recognized as the world's number one driver.

After a series of remarkable drives in less than fully competitive cars in the 1930s, Wimille spent World War II as a member of the French Resistance. Returning to racing after the war, he finally got his hands on machinery worthy of his abilities in the early post-war years, when he was recruited by the dominant Alfa Romeo team.

In 1947 and 1948, he was clearly the quickest man in a squad that included the legendary Achille Varzi. He won the French and Italian Grand Prix in 1948 and, had there been a World Championship at that time, there is no doubt that Wimille would have taken the crown.

He crashed his Simca-Gordini into a tree on his third lap of practice for the 1949 Perón Grand Prix in Argentina,

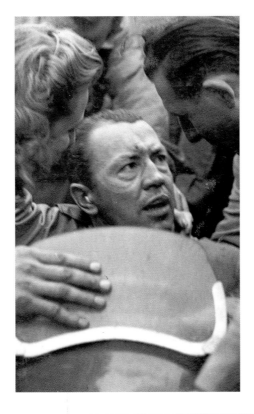

Jean-Pierre Wimille	
Nationality	French
Seasons	1930–48
Teams driven for	Bugatti, Alfa Romeo
Number of major victories	4

with fatal consequences. It was believed that the early morning sun had blinded him. Bizarrely, it was the first time Wimille had ever worn a crash helmet.

◄ Jean-Pierre Wimille. The Frenchman was widely regarded as the world's greatest driver during the late 1940s.

▼ Wimille in the Alfa 158 at the Grand Prix of the Nations, Geneva, Switzerland, in 1946.

A–Z
Constructors

In 1895, Panhard-Levassor took one of the pioneering, new-fangled motor cars it was trying to sell to the public, and modified it with an override switch on its engine-speed governer. Thus was created the first winning racing car.

Although a divergence quickly formed between road cars and racing machines, for many decades racing car constructors tended to be the same teams as those who built customer cars for the public. In the late 1920s, specialist teams began to form, relying on racing for their existence. Some, like *Scuderia Ferrari*, relied on the hardware of manufacturers. Others, like Maserati, began building their own machines. But still the factories were the dominant constructors.

But by the end of the 1950s, Formula One was being dominated by a new breed that were constructors in a more literal sense. Pioneered by Cooper, these teams assembled their cars using bought-in components. This formed the blueprint for Formula One constructors for the next 20 years. But with the commercial success of Formula One came the return of the big car-producing factories – but this time with a difference; they usually entered the sport in partnership with an existing specialist team.

This mix of specialist understanding with factory financial clout characterizes the Formula One constructor of today.

◄ The drama of the pit stop.
Mika Salo's Toyota lays rubber.

Alfa Romeo

◀ The Alfa 158 "Alfetta" was conceived pre-war as a voiturette racer but had a successful post-war career as a Championship Grand Prix winning car.

▼ Bruno Giocomelli's Alfa leads the 1980 USA Grand Prix. He was dominating the race until the coil failed at three-quarter distance.

Within months of producing its first road-going cars in 1910, this Turin-based company was involved in racing to publicize its products. It reached the front rank of the sport in the 1920s when, aided by one of its drivers, Enzo Ferrari, it poached key racing technical staff from the bigger Fiat concern.

Chief among these staff was the brilliant designer, Vittorio Jano, who created the company's first successful Grand Prix car, the P2. Introduced in 1924, it won the inaugural World Manufacturers' Championship the following year. Jano's P3 of 1930 was the first genuine single-seater Grand Prix car and remained successful for many years, sealing its immortality

Alfa Romeo	
Country of origin	Italy
Date of foundation	1910
Active years in Grands Prix	1924–39, 1946–51, 1979–85
Grand Prix victories	10 (+ 42 pre-championship)

when Tazio Nuvolari took it to victory against the far more advanced German cars in the 1935 German Grand Prix.

The German domination eventually led to Alfa concentrating on voiturette ("small car") racing in the late 1930s, with an elegant 1.5-litre machine dubbed the "Alfetta". Designed by Giocchino Colombo under the direction of Alfa's now racing manager, Enzo Ferrari, it got a new lease of life post World War II when Formula One

was created along the lines of the old voiturette formula. It won Giuseppe Farina the inaugural World Drivers' Championship in 1950, with team-mate Juan Manuel Fangio following up with the 1951 title.

Thereafter the company withdrew from Formula One. It returned as an engine supplier to Brabham in 1976 before committing itself to an unsuccessful constructors role from 1979 to 1985.

Auto Union

This company was created in 1932 with the merger of four German car manufacturers. Its boss, Baron Klaus van Oertzen, was a racing fan and took the company into Grand Prix racing after the Nazi party offered subsidies for any company representing the Fatherland in the sport.

Van Oertzen commissioned former Mercedes engineer Ferdinand Porsche to design a car for the new 750kg formula of 1934, and he came up with a stunning mid-engined V16 design. Like the rival Mercedes, its independent suspension was a novelty and proved to be the trigger that allowed previously unheard of horsepower to be utilized. Hans Stuck won races in the car's first season and a development of it dominated 1936 with Bernd Rosemeyer. When the latter driver was

Auto Union	
Country of origin	Germany
Date of foundation	1932
Active years in Grands Prix	1934–39
Grand Prix victories	15 pre-championship

killed attempting a world speed record for the company, he was replaced by the legendary Tazio Nuvolari, who enjoyed much success in 1938 and 1939 in new V12 supercharged versions.

However, World War II left the constituent parts of the company in different countries, under different regimes, splitting it up. Today's Audi is one of the descendants.

▲ H. P. Muller in an Auto Union V16 during the European Mountain Championship round at Grossglockner in 1939.

► Tazio Nuvolari in action at Donington Park, England, in 1938, winning the 250-mile International Grand Prix at an average speed of 129.53km/h (80.49mph).

Ballot

▼ Ernest Ballot oversees preparation of his team cars in the pits, 1921.

The French Ballot company made its mark in the sport first in the American Indianapolis 500 race, and subsequently in Grand Prix racing, in the early 1920s.

Founded by Ernest Ballot, a French maritime engineer who had been producing road-going engines, the company switched to production of Hispano-Suiza V8 aero engines during World War I. This accelerated the company's understanding of engine technology and, encouraged by racing driver René Thomas, Ballot branched out into the manufacture of racing cars in 1919. For this, the company employed designer Ernest Henry, who had been responsible for the first twin-cam Grand Prix car, the 1912 Peugeot.

Henry's new design proved to be the pacesetter at Indianapolis for several years in succession, beginning in 1919, though appalling luck meant it never did win the event. An adaptation of this car won the 1921 Brescia Grand Prix with former Peugeot driver Jules Goux, but this was the company's final moment of glory within the sport. Henry was recruited by the rival Sunbeam concern and Ballot withdrew.

It thereafter concentrated on production cars until being bought out in the early 1930s by the same Hispano-Suiza company for which it had built aero engines during the war. Shortly afterwards, founder Ernest Ballot was dismissed.

▲ Ballot adapted its Indianapolis car for Grand Prix racing in 1921.

◄ Ballots were the fastest cars at the Indianapolis 500 from 1919 to 1922 but failed to win the event.

Ballot	
Country of origin	France
Date of foundation	1906
Active years in Grands Prix	1919–22
Grand Prix victories	1 pre-championship

Benetton

▼ **Gerhard Berger gives Benetton its first Grand Prix victory at Mexico in 1986.**

The famous Italian fashion clothes manufacturer first appeared in Formula One as a sponsor of the British Tyrrell team in 1983; founder Luciano Benetton was attracted by the image-boosting profile of the sport.

After a further spell sponsoring the Alfa Romeo team, Benetton decided to become a Formula One constructor in its own right when the opportunity of purchasing the British former Toleman team presented itself in time for the 1986 season. This, it was felt, represented better value than simply being a sponsor, and the team itself was already up and running. The resident designer Rory Byrne proved himself a highly gifted man and his BMW turbo-powered B186 was competitive enough to give the team – and its driver Gerhard Berger – their first Grand Prix success at Mexico 1986.

Sporadic success followed until the team was put on a more solid footing with the recruitment in 1989 of Flavio Briatore, a friend and business associate of Luciano Benetton. In partnership with Ford, competitiveness grew. For 1990, racing entrepreneur Tom Walkinshaw bought a share in the team, bringing with him designer Ross Brawn. Although Walkinshaw subsequently left, the technical partnership of Brawn and Byrne proved exceptionally fertile, especially so when blended with the driving gifts of the startling newcomer Michael Schumacher. The German won his first Grand Prix for the team in 1992, and two years later

Benetton

Country of origin	United Kingdom
Date of foundation	1986
Active years in Grands Prix	1986–2001
Grand Prix victories	27 (+ 1 Constructors' Cup)

the team secured the World Drivers' Championship. This feat was repeated in 1995, this time with Renault power in place of Ford.

For the 1996 season, Schumacher left Benetton for Ferrari, and within a year Brawn and Byrne had followed him there. This rather decimated the team, despite the return of Gerhard Berger. The Austrian took Benetton's final Grand Prix victory at Hockenheim in 1997. The team continued for another four years, but in 2000 it was bought by Renault. In 2002, the Benetton tag was dropped in favour of the name of the parent company. The Renault Formula One cars are still built in the former Benetton premises in England.

◄ **Michael Schumacher celebrates victory in the 1995 Pacific Grand Prix.**

▼ **Schumacher's 1995 win at Aida clinches Benetton's second successive championship.**

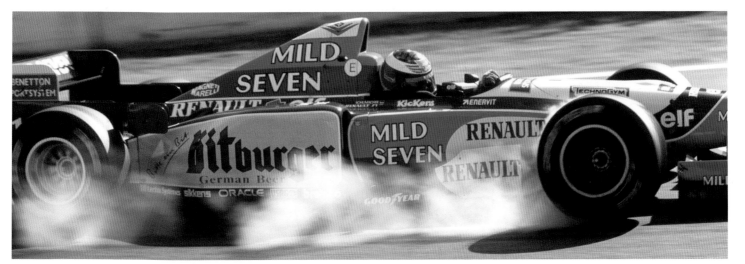

Brabham

After winning two World Championships with Cooper in 1959 and 1960, Jack Brabham found the team's impetus running out in the seasons that followed. For 1962, he decided to branch out on his own, and his Brabham team became one of the core British teams – using bought-in components in the way Cooper had pioneered – that came to dominate the sport in that era.

Brabham initially built customer racing cars for the lower formulae, partly to fund the Formula One team. The cars were all designed by Ron Tauranac, a friend of Jack Brabham's from their days in Australian dirt-track racing. They soon proved highly effective. Dan Gurney gave the team its first Grand Prix victory in France in 1964. In the same country two years later, Jack became the first man to win a Grand Prix in a car bearing his own name. This was the foundation for winning the World Drivers' and Constructors' Championships of that year. In 1967, Brabham's second driver Denny Hulme gave the team its second successive championship double.

▼ Jack Brabham at the 1966 French Grand Prix, becoming the first man to win in a car bearing his own name.

◄ The Brabham BT3 made its Grand Prix debut in the hands of the team owner, Jack Brabham. He retired on lap nine of the 1962 German Grand Prix with a broken throttle linkage.

Brabham retired at the end of 1970, and returned home to Australia. The team was initially bought by Tauranac, but soon after it was sold again, this time to Bernie Ecclestone, who had managed the late Jochen Rindt, a former Brabham driver. Ecclestone gave the team a new lease of life, aided by the brilliant young South African designer, Gordon Murray.

In winning the 1981 world title, Nelson Piquet gave the Ecclestone-era Brabham its first title success. It was a feat the team repeated in 1983, this time in partnership with BMW. This association saw Brabham pioneer the use of electronic engine management and pits-to-car telemetry. Furthermore, in 1982, Murray re-introduced the tactical pit stop to Formula One racing, after a gap of three decades.

Ecclestone sold the team in 1987. It stuttered on, ever less successful, until going out of business in 1992.

Brabham	
Country of origin	United Kingdom
Date of foundation	1962
Active years in Grands Prix	1962–92
Grand Prix victories	35 (+ 1 Constructors' Cup)

◄ Brabham reintroduced tactical pit stops to Formula One, as here, with Nelson Piquet making a stop at Silverstone in 1983.

BRM

British Racing Motors was the brainchild of Raymond Mays, a successful racing driver of the 1930s, who had also initiated the ERA company of that time. With the post-war BRM project, Mays devised the idea of a motor racing trust, with financial and resource contributions from British industry. The resulting car would advertise British engineering excellence to the rest of the world through the medium of Formula One racing. To this end, designer Peter Berthon came up with a hugely complex machine, with an engine of 16 tiny cylinders, which complied with the 1.5-litre supercharged regulations for Formula One.

The engine was said to have a power potential of up to 600bhp, which, if true, would have made it a match for the all-conquering Alfettas of the time. Unfortunately, the car proved horrifically unreliable and, after interminable delays, it fell into obsolescence when the technical regulations were changed. What had been billed as a world-beater became a laughing stock.

In the mid-1950s, industrialist Alfred Owen bought out the company, retaining Mays as a consultant. For the 2.5-litre formula a much simpler car, the P25, was built, and Jo Bonnier won the team's first Grand Prix in Holland 1959. The 1.5-litre formula of 1961–65 marked the team's glory years. With the

▲ **Graham Hill, here in the 1962 French Grand Prix, gave BRM its one and only world title in 27 years of trying.**

BRM

Country of origin	United Kingdom
Date of foundation	1948
Active years in Grands Prix	1950–77
Grand Prix victories	17 (+ 1 Constructors' Cup)

▼ **Jo Siffert dominated the 1971 Austrian Grand Prix for BRM. It was the team's last fully competitive season.**

mid-engined V8 P57 of 1962, Graham Hill won the World Championship. In 1965 Jackie Stewart took his first Grand Prix victory with the team after a dramatic dice with team-mate Hill.

Early mistakes were repeated when the 3-litre formula was introduced in 1966, as the team produced a heavy and inefficient H16. A V12 engine originally designed for sports car racing brought a measure of respectability back to the team in the early 1970s, but by the middle part of that decade, the team – under the direction of Owen's brother-in-law Louis Stanley – was under-funded and lacking direction. Its last Grand Prix appearance came in 1977.

Bugatti

Ettore Bugatti was an eccentric self-trained Italian artist-cum-engineer who gave the world the fabulous and beautiful Bugatti line of cars, built in Molsheim in the Alsace region of France in the 1920s and 1930s. These were exquisite and exotic machines to which the rich and famous aspired. Ettore also designed and built devastatingly successful racing cars, notably the Type 35, introduced in 1924 and still winning Grands Prix in the early 1930s.

Before setting up Bugatti cars in 1910, Ettore had received commissions from manufacturers such as Peugeot and de Dietrich, and during World War I he designed a 16-cylinder aero engine, the internal design of which influenced racing car builders in the early 1920s. The Type 35 was the first truly successful Bugatti Grand Prix car, taken to major victories by a whole host of drivers. Its twin-cam derivative, the Type 51, continued the winning lineage. But the German domination of the mid-1930s left Bugatti unable to respond, at a time when it was going through internal difficulties.

▲ The type 59 model took over from the 35/51 late in 1933 but was soon overwhelmed by the new German cars.

◄ Driver Maurice Trintignant (in white hat and raincoat) at the new Bugatti T251 Formula One car tests in 1956.

Ettore's son Jean, a talented stylist for the company, was seen as Ettore's natural heir but was killed testing a sports car in 1939. Ettore himself died in 1947. The company continued from one financial crisis to another but managed to create a radical mid-engined Formula One car, the 251, in 1956. However, the car was under-developed and, ultimately, unsuccessful and the company died soon after.

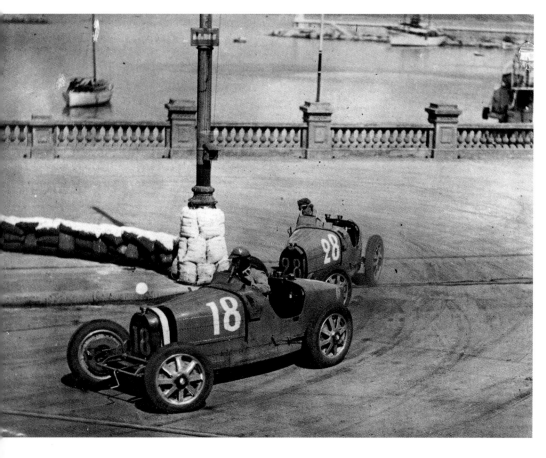

Bugatti	
Country of origin	France
Date of foundation	1909
Active years in Grands Prix	1921–39 and 1956
Grand Prix victories	35 pre-championship

◄ Bugatti's type 35/51 ran at the frontline of Grands Prix from 1924 until 1933. For a time the car formed the backbone of Grand Prix racing.

Connaught

A Connaught became the first British car ever to win a Formula One race when Tony Brooks took victory in the 1955 Syracuse Grand Prix, a non-championship event. It was also the first Formula One victory for a car equipped with disc brakes.

Rodney Clarke, a brilliant engineer, was the brains behind the Connaught team. Kenneth McAlpine, construction company heir and amateur racer, was the money. After beginning in British club racing in the early 1950s, Connaught graduated to Grand Prix when the World Championship was switched to Formula Two cars for 1952.

Lack of a suitable engine always

Connaught	
Country of origin	United Kingdom
Date of foundation	1949
Active years in Grands Prix	1952–58
Grand Prix victories	0 (1 non-championship)

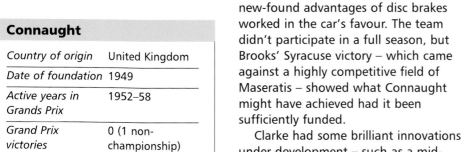

▼ Archie Scott-Brown showed the potential of the B-type Connaught in several British non-championship races.

hindered the company upon the reintroduction of Formula One, but the quality of the chassis and the new-found advantages of disc brakes worked in the car's favour. The team didn't participate in a full season, but Brooks' Syracuse victory – which came against a highly competitive field of Maseratis – showed what Connaught might have achieved had it been sufficiently funded.

Clarke had some brilliant innovations under development – such as a mid-engined, monocoque construction car that was years ahead of its time. Partly due to Clarke's fastidious

▲ The A-type Connaught was a popular Formula Two car in the early 1950s. Here, Margulies in an example from 1951.

nature, such developments never saw the light of day, and the potential of this constructor was not widely seen. Its advanced philosophy was evident when it became the first Formula One team to have its own wind tunnel. But progress was slow, and, at the end of 1957, the company ceased to be as McAlpine tired of investing in it. Bernie Ecclestone bought some of the assets and made an ill-starred attempt to qualify for a couple of Grands Prix the following year, but the company itself was dead, a tale of unfulfilled potential.

Cooper

The Cooper team forever changed the convention of where a Formula One car's engine was situated – and a lot more besides. After a breakthrough victory with a tiny mid-engined car at the Argentina Grand Prix in 1958, the days of front-engined cars were numbered. It also heralded the domination of Formula One by specialist British assemblers, using bought-in components, making the sport less reliant on road car-producing factories.

Father and son Charles and John Cooper ran the team from a garage in Surbiton, near London. They initially set up in the early post-war years as manufacturers of cars for the then new Formula 500 series, a low-cost formula for cars powered by 500cc motorcycle engines. With engines designed for chain-drive, the logical place to put the engine was in between the driver and the rear wheels. The Coopers took this F500 convention all the way to Formula One, the breakthrough for them being when engine suppliers Coventry Climax came up with a twin-cam engine, giving the Cooper reasonable power for the first time.

Jack Brabham took works Cooper-Climaxes to victory in both the 1959 and 1960 World Championships, and Formula One changed forever. No

▲ In winning the 1960 British Grand Prix, Jack Brabham put Cooper well on the way to its successive World Championship.

Cooper	
Country of origin	United Kingdom
Date of foundation	1948
Active years in Grands Prix	1952–68
Grand Prix victories	16 (+ 2 Constructors' Cups)

▼ Cooper's final race victory came with Pedro Rodriguez in 1967 in South Africa.

longer would the sport's health be at the whim of road car manufacturers, as Cooper's method divorced the technicalities of the cars from road car convention, and at the same time opened up Formula One to specialists lacking the financial resource to fund engine design and build programmes.

Ironically, other British specialist constructors created in a similar vein, such as Lotus, Brabham and McLaren – the latter two companies created by former works Cooper drivers – leapfrogged Cooper. Using Maserati engines, the team took its final race victory with Pedro Rodriguez in South Africa in 1967, and withdrew at the end of the following year.

Delage

This French constructor sealed its place of immortality within the sport when, in 1927, it won all four major Grands Prix comprising the season, with its lead driver Robert Benoist.

Founded in 1905 by Louis Delage, the former chief of development at Peugeot, the company began by producing road-going cars. It then entered voiturette ("small car") racing for publicity. The company's first Grand Prix car came in 1912, and was highly sophisticated for the time, with desmodronic valve actuation and a five-speed gearbox. Two years later, René Thomas took a Delage to victory in the Indianapolis 500.

Delage

Country of origin	France
Date of foundation	1905
Active years in Grands Prix	1912–27
Grand Prix victories	7 pre-championship

Grand Prix success came in the 1920s, first with a V12-engined car and later with the straight-8 that came to dominate in 1927. However, the development costs of these cars came close to bankrupting the company and it withdrew from the sport. It was later bought-out by Delahaye, and Louis Delage was pensioned off. He died in relative poverty in 1947.

▲ Robert Benoist in the 1924 French Grand Prix held in Lyons. He drove the 2-litre V-12 Delage 2LCV to third place. Note the driver's protective face mask.

▼ The Delage 1.5 litre model in action at the 1927 British Grand Prix at Brooklands.

Duesenberg

By winning the French Grand Prix in 1921, Jimmy Murphy made Duesenberg the first American manufacturer to triumph in a major European race. But the company's racing credentials had already been established by success in America, notably the Indianapolis 500. The cars were the beautifully-engineered creations of the brothers Fred and August Duesenberg. Unusually, they began in racing before diversifying into road car production, with some of the most luxurious and sought-after machines of the 1920s and 1930s.

Divergence in technical regulation between American and European racing after 1921 meant that Duesenberg did not stay around to build on its successful European foray, and instead went on to dominate the Indy 500.

Duesenberg

Country of origin	USA
Date of foundation	1914
Active years in Grands Prix	1921
Grand Prix victories	1 pre-championship

▲ *(top)* The Deusenbergs shocked France by winning the French Grand Prix at Le Mans in 1921.

▲ *(above)* Jimmy Murphy in a Deusenberg at the French Grand Prix, Le Mans, 1921.

◄ Tommy Milton in a Duesenberg at Indianapolis in 1920.

Ferrari

E nzo Ferrari had been a works driver with Alfa Romeo in the early 1920s, and subsequently became its general "fixer", recruiting key technical staff from Fiat, for example. He took an Alfa Romeo dealership and formed a race team, Scuderia Ferrari, which for a time became the official race entrant of Alfa Romeo. He finally split from Alfa in 1939, with the intention of building his own cars.

In 1948, the first Grand Prix Ferrari appeared. It enjoyed some success in 1949, but this was largely due to the absence of the previously dominant Alfa Romeo. When the latter team returned in 1950, Ferrari was again reduced to also-ran status. The breakthrough came the following year, when Ferrari's designer Aurelio Lampredi came up with a 4.5-litre normally-aspirated car that, through its fuel-thriftiness, was able to defeat the supercharged Alfas at the British Grand Prix, driven by José Froilán González.

The first World Championships came in 1952 and 1953 with Alberto Ascari, and there followed further titles for Juan Manuel Fangio in 1956 and Mike Hawthorn in 1958. A new 1.5-litre formula for 1961 saw Ferrari more prepared than anyone else and the red cars dominated the championship, driven by Phil Hill and Wolfgang von Trips. John Surtees took another title for the team in 1964. There was then a barren period until the mid-1970s, when the combined forces of designer Mauro Forghieri and driver Niki Lauda brought a four-year sequence of victories

◀ The Monaco Grand Prix was one of five victories that Niki Lauda took in 1975 on his way to the first Ferrari World Championship for 11 years.

Ferrari	
Country of origin	Italy
Date of foundation	1946
Active years in Grands Prix	1948–present
Grand Prix victories	166 (+ 13 Constructors' Cups)

that yielded two Drivers' and three Constructors' World Championships.

Jody Scheckter and Gilles Villeneuve brought the team another Constructors' title in 1979, with Scheckter also taking the Drivers' honours. Ferrari then took the 1982 and 1983 Constructors' Championships before another barren period, as the British teams overtook them in the depth of their technology.

Enzo died in 1988, after which the team came under the full control of Fiat, which had bought into it in 1969. A period of success came in 1989–90, with innovative John Barnard-designed cars, whose chassis were conceived and built in Britain, but it was the arrival of former manager Luca di Montezemolo in 1991 that led to more sustained success – and with cars that were once more of Italian manufacture.

Michael Schumacher joined in 1996, and with the arrival of his Benetton technical partners, Ross Brawn and Rory Byrne, a new era of success dawned. They took a close championship win in 2000, and dominated in 2001 and 2002. A record-breaking fifth consecutive world constructors' title came in 2003.

▼ Michael Schumacher's victory in the 2002 British Grand Prix helped Ferrari to its fourth consecutive constructors' title.

Fiat

▼ Felice Nazzaro driving for Fiat at Targa Florio in 1907.

R ight from its birth at the turn of the 20th century, the Milan-based Fiat concern saw racing as essential to its image and its technical education. It graduated to international motor racing in 1904 and its ambitious philosophy was demonstrated when it pioneered the progression from side-valve to overhead-valve engines. It was later an early convert to the overhead-camshaft motor.

In 1907, Fiat won all three major races of the season with their lead driver Felice Nazzaro, backed up by Vincenzo Lancia, both of whom had been inherited when Fiat bought the Ceirano company in 1900. Fiat remained a major force in Grand Prix racing up until the outbreak of World War I.

Newly informed by the technology drive of war, Fiat again set the technological pace in the early 1920s, thanks to a brilliant group of engineers, directed by Guido Fornaca but also including Vittorio Jano. The philosophy

Fiat

Country of origin	Italy
Date of foundation	1900
Active years in Grands Prix	1904–24 and 1927
Grand Prix victories	12 pre-championship

behind their straight-eight engine of 1921 proved highly influential for decades to come. Fiat was the dominant Grand Prix force in 1922 and 1923 (when it was the first to win a Grand Prix with a supercharged engine), but by 1924 rival teams had begun to poach its technical staff. This triggered the company's withdrawal at the end of the year. It made a brief –

and victorious – comeback in 1927, but generally concentrated on its production range thereafter. In 1969, the company acquired Ferrari as one of its specialist satellites.

▼ David Bruce-Brown in his Fiat 14.1-litre model at the 1912 French Grand Prix at Dieppe.

Hesketh

▼ James Hunt ended his and Hesketh's first year of Formula One with second place and a lap record in the USA Grand Prix.

The British Lord, Alexander Hesketh, brightened up the Formula One scene in the mid-1970s with his eccentric but successful team that was built around the talents of designer Dr Harvey Postlethwaite and leading driver James Hunt.

Hesketh himself projected the image an of an aristocratic dilettante – and his team remains the only one to have included a grand piano as part of its race weekend cargo – but Postlethwaite and Hunt were gifted and committed. The three parties found themselves thrown together by circumstance. Separately, neither Hesketh nor Hunt had enjoyed great success in the junior categories of the sport but decided to graduate to Formula One together in 1973. To this end, a car was purchased from the March team, and with it came promising March boffin, Postlethwaite.

With Postlethwaite's modifications, the March performed far better than the similar cars of the works team, culminating in second place and a lap record for Hunt in the 1973 American

▼ James Hunt ended his and Hesketh's first year of Formula One with second place and a lap record in the USA Grand Prix.

Grand Prix. For the following year Postlethwaite designed a new "Hesketh" car. At the 1975 Dutch Grand Prix Hunt took the Hesketh to a fairy tale victory over the mighty Ferrari of that year's World Champion, Niki Lauda.

But it was close to the final hurrah. Even a Lord didn't have money to burn indefinitely and, with no significant commercial backers, the team released Hunt and Postlethwaite and resorted to running pay-drivers for a further couple of seasons before pulling out completely.

Hesketh

Country of origin	United Kingdom
Date of foundation	1972
Active years in Grands Prix	1973–78
Grand Prix victories	1

▼ Hunt withstood pressure from Lauda's Ferrari to win the 1975 Dutch Grand Prix.

Jordan

▼ Damon Hill gave Jordan its first Grand Prix victory at a wet 1998 Belgian Grand Prix.

Guided by the entrepreneurial Irishman Eddie Jordan, this team made what seemed at the time to be a financially suicidal bid to graduate to Formula One in 1991, and, remarkably, they made it work.

With lots of wheeling and dealing and a very respectable car from designer Gary Anderson, Jordan made its mark during its first Formula One season of 1991 after a successful decade in the junior ranks of Formula Three and Formula 3000. In between scoring points that took them to fifth place in the Constructors' Championship, Jordan took a lap record in Hungary, had one of its drivers, Bertrand Gachot, jailed for assault, introduced Formula One to the talents of Michael Schumacher – and then immediately lost him to a bigger team.

Hovering for the first few years on the brink of financial disaster, Jordan steadily built itself up, helped by partnerships first with Yamaha then Peugeot. Rubens Barrichello gave the team its first pole position at Spa in 1994. Four years later this was the

◄ Giancarlo Fisichella won the team's fourth victory in the rain of Brazil in 2003.

venue of Jordan's first Grand Prix victory, as Damon Hill and Ralf Schumacher drove their Mugen-Honda-powered cars to a Jordan 1-2.

Heinz-Harald Frentzen scored two further victories for the team in 1999 and was an outside championship contender until the penultimate race of the season. The team has never been quite able to repeat such form but it remains one of the sport's most high-profile and imaginative participants.

Jordan	
Country of origin	United Kingdom
Date of foundation	1991
Active years in Grands Prix	1991–present
Grand Prix victories	4

◄ Bertrand Gachot giving the Jordan team its Formula One baptism at the 1991 USA Grand Prix in Phoenix, Arizona.

Lancia

▼ Alberto Ascari won the 1955 non-championship Valentino Grand Prix, the Lancia team's only victory.

Founded by former Fiat racer Vincenzo Lancia in 1906, this company initially concentrated on road-going cars. By the time it first entered Grand Prix racing in 1954, Vincenzo's son Gianni was running it.

Gianni Lancia commissioned legendary design genius Vittorio Jano to create a car for the new 2.5-litre Formula One regulations of 1954. This machine, dubbed the D50, showed beyond doubt that the elderly Jano's creative flair was still very much intact. He favoured an engine with the then highly unusual V8 format and used it to form part of the car's structural stiffness – the first time this had been done in Formula One and not to be seen again for another 12 years. He also gave the car long and low pannier fuel tanks, separate from the main

body, keeping changes in the centre of gravity to a minimum as the fuel load decreased.

Alberto Ascari gave this car its debut at the 1954 Spanish Grand Prix, the final race of the season, and set pole position by over a second. He was leading the race comfortably when the car broke down. Lancia began 1955 as joint favourites with Mercedes for the world title, but financial problems and the death of Ascari in a testing accident with Ferrari meant it all turned sour. Lancia withdrew at the end of the year, never to return. The assets of the Grand Prix project were then handed over to

Ferrari, who, using modified versions of the D50, dominated the 1956 World Championship. The cars continued into 1957 before being replaced by a model of Ferrari's own design.

▲ Ferrari used the Lancia D50 to win the 1956 World Championship with Fangio.

Lancia	
Country of origin	Italy
Date of foundation	1906
Active years in Grands Prix	1954–55
Grand Prix victories	0 (1 non-championship)

► The 1954 Lancia D50 was the most technically advanced car of its time, but its full potential was never realized.

Ligier

▼ Jacques Lafitte got Ligier off to a flying start in 1979 with victories in the first two races of the season.

This all-French team entered Grand Prix racing in 1976 after serving its apprenticeship in sports car racing. It was the project of Guy Ligier, a colourful character who had been a rugby international as well as a privateer Formula One driver in the 1960s.

Backed by French tobacco company Gitanes and using the Matra V12 engine, Ligier enjoyed a surprisingly competitive first season, thanks largely to the design talents of former Matra engineer Gerard Ducarouge and the driving of Jacques Laffite. Together they won their first Grand Prix in Sweden 1977.

A switch to the Cosworth DFV engine and a superb new ground-effect chassis from Ducarouge gave the team a fantastic start to 1979, as Laffite dominated the opening two races. Team-mate Patrick Depailler then won in Spain and at the halfway point of the year both drivers were in contention for the championship. But Depailler was then injured and the car lost its form, leaving Laffite fourth in the championship. Further success came in 1980, Laffite and Didier Pironi often showing the

Ligier	
Country of origin	France
Date of foundation	1970
Active years in Grands Prix	1976–97
Grand Prix victories	9

▼ Lafitte in the first Formula One Ligier "teapot" taking fourth place at the USA Grand Prix West, Long Beach, in 1976. This was the team's first points finish.

JS11/15 model to be the fastest around, but consistency again proved elusive. Laffite was a championship contender in 1981, now with Matra power once more, but again ended up fourth.

A liaison with road car producer Talbot lasted from 1981 until the end of 1982 after which the glory days of the team were effectively over. It went through several changes of ownership and even won one more race – with Olivier Panis at Monaco 1996 – but was never again a competitive force. At the end of 1996 the team was acquired by Alain Prost and renamed after him.

Lotus

C olin Chapman was the founding genius of Lotus, arguably the most influential and innovative team in Grand Prix history.

The team entered Formula One in 1958, and Stirling Moss took the marque's first victory at Monaco in 1960 in a car privately owned and entered by Rob Walker. Shortly afterwards, Moss was badly injured when his suspension broke at Spa, and a reputation of frailty would dog Lotus for much of the next couple of decades. The cars tended to either break or win.

The Lotus 25 of 1962 was the first Formula One car to feature monocoque construction. Jim Clark took it to Lotus' first World Championship in 1963 and followed it up with another in 1965, while a development of the car also won Clark the Indy 500 that year.

The Lotus 49 of 1967 used the new Cosworth DFV engine as a structural part of the car, another highly progressive feature. Small winglets and an upward-sweeping rear body on this car at Monaco in 1968 signalled the arrival of downforce in Formula One. Within a few races most of the field carried huge front and rear wings on stilts. The wedge-shaped Lotus 72 of 1970 resolved the conflicting requirements of downforce and low drag. The Lotus 78 of 1977 brought another quantum leap in aerodynamic downforce through the application of the ground-effect principle. The follow-up Lotus 79 dominated the 1978 World Championship. Five drivers – Clark, Graham Hill, Jochen Rindt, Emerson Fittipaldi and Mario Andretti – won world titles with Lotus.

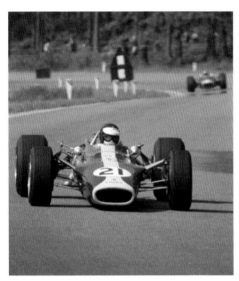

▲ Jim Clark, here in the 1967 Belgian Grand Prix, won two World Championship titles for the Lotus team.

Lotus	
Country of origin	United Kingdom
Date of foundation	1956
Active years in Grands Prix	1958–94
Grand Prix victories	79 (+ 7 Constructors' Cups)

Chapman died from a heart attack late in 1982. The team never fully recovered, though it did subsequently enjoy a spell of success with Ayrton Senna in a Renault turbo-engined car. The last win came at Detroit in 1987. Once Senna left, success dried up, and the team went downhill before going out of business at the end of 1994.

▼ The Lotus 78 of 1977 introduced the ground-effect concept to Formula One.

Maserati

Alfieri Maserati was the guiding force behind this specialist race car constructor, aided by four of his brothers. He established his Bologna garage and tuning business in 1914 but didn't build a "Maserati" car until 1926. This was when the Diatto company, which had commissioned him to design and build them a Grand Prix car, got into financial trouble, leaving him to take over the project. A gifted driver as well as engineer, Alfieri scored well with the car. Developments of it were ever-more competitive and by the early 1930s, Maserati was enjoying considerable success with drivers such as Achille Varzi and Tazio Nuvolari. Alfieri himself died in 1932 from a prostrate injury he received while racing, leaving the running of the business to brother Bindo.

The German domination of the mid- to late-1930s led Maserati to leave Grand Prix racing and compete instead in the voiturette ("small car") category. After World War II, this became Formula One, bringing Maserati back into Grand Prix competition. By this time, the company had been bought out by the Orsi family and relocated to Modena. After serving a

10-year service contract, the Maserati brothers left in 1947 and founded a new racing outfit, OSCA.

Maserati hardware formed the mainstay of early post-war racing as their cars proved highly popular with privateers. The works team enjoyed

Maserati	
Country of origin	Italy
Date of foundation	1926
Active years in Grands Prix	1926–39, 1946–58
Grand Prix victories	9 (+ 11 pre-championship)

considerable success in the pre-World Championship era with Alberto Ascari and Luigi Villoresi. It wasn't until 1953 that the team scored its first championship-status Grand Prix victory, with Juan Manuel Fangio in Italy.

For 1954's 2.5-litre formula, Maserati designer Giocchino Colombo designed the 250F. It won races immediately and, although it did not take the title until 1957, the car established itself as one of the all-time greats. Maserati was in financial difficulty by 1958 and withdrew from the sport to concentrate on the production of its exotic road-going sports cars, a line initiated by the Orsis earlier in the decade.

▲ The 1926 Maserati type 26.

◄ Juan Manuel Fangio in the Maserati 250F. The Argentinian ace served two spells with Maserati from 1952–1954 and 1957–1958. He took Maserati's first and only World Championship win in 1957.

Matra

This French missile manufacturer entered the sport in 1964 when it took over the ailing Bonett sports car constructor, the founder of which was a friend of Matra chief, Marcel Chassagny.

Matra put engineer Jean-Luc Lagardère in charge of the new subsidiary and he enthusiastically committed to a long-term programme of competition, comprising Formula Three, Formula Two, and eventual graduation to Formula One. Backed by Elf, this came in 1968. The company had designed a new V12 engine for the project but hedged its bets by supplying a car to Ken Tyrrell, who fitted it with the dominant Ford Cosworth DFV V8 and had it driven by Jackie Stewart. The Cosworth-engined car proved more competitive than the Matra-powered one and Stewart only narrowly missed out on the World Championship that year.

For 1969 Matra withdrew its own team to further develop the V12, but Stewart and Tyrrell enjoyed a dominant season in the Matra-Ford, making Matra World Constructors' Champion in only its second year of Formula One. Ironically, it proved to be the team's final flourish of Formual One success.

A marketing tie-up with Chrysler France for a road car made the Matra-Ford politically unacceptable, and the Tyrrell arrangement came to an end.

▼ A puncture deprived Chris Amon's Matra MS120D of victory in France in 1972.

▲ Jackie Stewart scored his fourth victory in five races in a Matra 1–2 finish at the French Grand Prix, Clermont Ferrand, 1969.

▼ Jean-Pierre Beltoise sits on the grid and finished in ninth place at the French Grand Prix, Rouen-les-Essarts, 1968.

Matra

Matra	
Country of origin	France
Date of foundation	1964
Active years in Grands Prix	1968–72
Grand Prix victories	9 (+ 1 Constructors' Cup)

Matra reintroduced its V12 engine but despite several competitive showings from 1970–72, it failed to win a Grand Prix. The company withdrew from the category at the end of 1972 to focus on sports car racing. Some years later, the V12 Matra engine got a taste of Formula One success, powering Jacques Laffite's Ligier to victories on three occasions between 1977 and 1981.

Mercedes

▼ German constructors Mercedes and Auto Union together dominated Grand Prix racing from 1934–39.

ottlieb Daimler is co-credited with the invention of the motor car. He did not live to see the completion of the "Mercedes" model he was working on at the turn of the century. Mercedes was the name of the daughter of Emile Julinek, the Austrian importer for the company. The car's name change from Daimler came in recognition of how big a progression this 1901 model was over anything previously seen. When Mercedes officially entered competition in 1903, it quickly ended the domination of the French Panhard and Mors marques.

The company regularly came in and out of the sport as it developed new technologies that fed its production car and aero-engine programmes. It was the first team to race an overhead-cam engined car, in 1906, and it won the French Grand Prix of 1908 and 1914.

In 1923, Mercedes introduced the supercharger to racing but its next period of sustained success didn't come until the inauguration of the 750kg

Mercedes	
Country of origin	Germany
Date of foundation	1901
Active years in Grands Prix	1903–08, 1914, 1926–39, 1954–55
Grand Prix victories	9 (+ 29 pre-championship)

formula of 1934 when, with Nazi party backing, Mercedes rewrote the rules of Grand Prix technology. With ever-more powerful cars that were soon reaching over 322km/h (200mph), the "silver arrows" – so named because of their bare aluminium bodies – dominated until the outbreak of World War Two.

It was 1954 before the company re-entered Grand Prix racing. It did so with the highly progressive W196, with Juan Manuel Fangio taking the car to victory on its debut in France. Fangio and Mercedes took the World title that year, and in 1955. Indeed, during two seasons of racing, the W196 was beaten on only three occasions. But at the end of the 1955 season, the company was forced to withdraw from the sport after one of its cars was launched into the crowd at the Le Mans 24 Hours sports car race, killing more than 80 of the spectators.

Following that catastrophe, it was to be a very long time before the company felt comfortable re-entering the sport. It did so first in sports car racing in the late 1980s, before entering Formula One with Sauber from 1993. After two years it switched its engine supply to the long-established McLaren team, and eventually this became one of the sport's greatest liaisons. McLaren-Mercedes dominated Formula One in 1998 and 1999, and continues to be a major force.

◄ Mercedes-Benz team-mates Stirling Moss (6) and Juan Manuel Fangio (2) lead the 1955 Monaco Grand Prix into the first corner.

Mors

Mors was one of the most successful pioneer racing manufacturers at the dawn of the sport in the late 19th and early 20th centuries.

Emile Mors, chief of one of France's leading telegraph equipment companies, founded the company in the 1890s and competed himself in some of the early city-to-city races. An injury in one of these events caused him to retire from competitive driving, but he employed others to do so for him. Using ever-more monstrous engines, Mors came to vie with Panhard as the fastest racing car of them all.

The Mors of Fernand Gabriel was victorious in the tragic Paris–Madrid

Mors	
Country of origin	France
Date of foundation	1897
Active years in Grands Prix	1897–1908
Grand Prix victories	11 pre-championship

race, in 1903, that caused city-to-city racing to be banned for all time. It was never to win a major event again. Mors built its last Grand Prix racing car in 1908 after failing to keep pace with technology advances introduced by more progressively engineered cars from the likes of Mercedes, Renault and Fiat. The company was later bought out by Citroën.

▲ *(right)* The 1902 Paris–Vienna type Mors, drivern by Augières at Archères, near Paris. He set a new land speed record of 123.4km/h (77.13mph).

▶ The 1903 Mors "Dauphin" shows an early attempt at steamlining.

McLaren

Kiwi Bruce McLaren left Cooper to form his own team in 1966. Within two years he had joined his former Cooper team-mate Jack Brabham in the exclusive club of men who have won Grands Prix in cars bearing their own name.

Tragically, Bruce never lived to see the colossus that his team came to be. He was killed testing a Can-Am sports car at Goodwood in 1970. His partner Teddy Mayer took over the running of the team – which was highly successful in Indycar and Can-Am racing, as well as Formula One – and steered it to its first World Championship, in 1974, with Emerson Fittipaldi and the Gordon Coppuck-designed M23 model. Two years later, James Hunt used an M23 in his dramatic title victory over Niki Lauda.

By the late 1970s, the team had lost its technical impetus, and its sponsor

◄ Bruce McLaren – here in third place – eventually won this race at Spa in 1968 for the team's first Formula One victory.

Marlboro arranged for a merger between McLaren and Marlboro's Formula Two team, Project 4, run by Ron Dennis. Dennis brought with him designer John Barnard who then produced the first carbon-fibre Formula One car, the McLaren MP4/1. This won a race in its first season and established the new era McLaren as a serious competitive force. World Championships

followed with TAG-Porsche power in 1984, 1985 and 1986, and with Honda in 1988, 1989, 1990 and 1991. During the 1980s and 1990s McLaren, together with Williams, dominated the sport, with Niki Lauda, Alain Prost and Ayrton Senna bringing championship glory to the team. A new partnership with Mercedes yielded titles in 1998 and 1999 with Mika Häkkinen. Since Häkkinen's retirement at the end of 2001, another Finn, Kimi Raikkonen, has led the team.

◄ Mika Häkkinen won the 1998 Monaco Grand Prix on his way to his first, and the team's tenth, drivers' title.

▼ Ayrton Senna leads eventual winner Alain Prost in the 1988 French Grand Prix. Their MP4/4s won 15 out of 16 races that year.

McLaren

Country of origin	United Kingdom
Date of foundation	1966
Active years in Grands Prix	1966–present
Grand Prix victories	137 (+ 8 Constructors' Cups)

Panhard

A Panhard-Levassor was the very first winning race car, taking the finish of the 1895 Paris–Bordeaux–Paris more than five hours ahead of its nearest competitor. It was driven by one of the partners in the business, Emile Levassor. The other partner was Louis-René Panhard.

A friend of Levassor's had gained the French commercial rights to the German Daimler engine, leading to Panhard and Levassor diversifying from their core engineering business to car manufacture. Racing was recognized as essential in both improving technology and advertising the capability of the automobile in general. Indeed, Emile Lavassor was one of the driving forces in the early days of the sport.

Using ever bigger, more powerful engines, Panhard dominated the early city-to-city events, though eventually it

began to be challenged hard by rival, Mors. Like that company, Panhard failed to keep up with advances introduced by more progressive companies and, again like Mors, it built its last Grand Prix racer in 1908, the year that Louis-René Panhard died. Thereafter, guided by Panhard's sons, it concentrated on production cars until the 1960s, when Citroën bought it out.

▲ The very first winning racing car won the 1895 Paris–Bordeaux–Paris race but wasn't eligible for the prize money on account of it having only two seats!

▼ Lebron's Panhard in the Circuit des Ardennes race in 1905.

Panhard	
Country of origin	France
Date of foundation	1895
Active years in Grands Prix	1895–1908
Grand Prix victories	22 pre-championship

▲ Henry Farman in a Panhard-Levassor passing through Criel-sur-Mer, Dieppe, in the 1908 French Grand Prix.

Peugeot

eugeot was already a very old company when the motor car was first invented, having begun as a steel works, producing everything from steel rods for insertion into fancy dresses to bicycles. It produced a steam car in 1889, but was soon converted to the benefits of the petrol engine by Gottlieb Daimler. Using Daimler-engined cars, Peugeot took part in the very first city-to-city races and later produced its own power units, designed by Louis Rigolout, who was also the company's nominated race driver.

Peugeot then lost interest in racing as it built up its production facilities. In 1906, a splinter group was formed, Lion-Peugeot, to produce bicycles and light cars. This company entered the new voiturette ("small car") class of racing, and became the dominant force there, with drivers Jules Goux, Georges Boillot and Paulo Zuccarelli. A 1911 reorganization brought the two companies back together and the racing core of the former offshoot planned its first full-size Grand Prix car. Designed by Ernest Henry, the 1912 Peugeot L76 model broke new technical ground in having twin overhead camshafts driving four valves for each engine cylinder.

It was a revolutionary concept, making up in technology what it conceded to its rivals in engine size – at 7.6 litres it was just over half the size of the 14.1-litre Fiat. After a closely matched race against the Fiat, Boillot took the car to victory in the 1912 French Grand Prix, and so brought the era of the racing monster to an end. Peugeot won again in 1913 and also took the American Indy 500 that year – something it repeated in 1916 and 1919. Henry left the company during

◀ Dario Resta won at Indianapolis for Peugeot in 1916. The progressive design of the car influenced a whole generation of imitators.

▼ (left) Goux took fourth at Indianapolis in 1914 but had won the event at his and Peugeot's first attempt in 1913.

▼ René Thomas in the Peugeot L3 won the Coupe de la Meuse at the Circuit des Ardennes, Belgium, in 1912. This car was a voiturette version of the Grand Prix car.

the war, Boillot was killed and then Goux departed too, leaving Peugeot bereft of racing experience. There was an attempt on the Indy 500 in 1921 with a radical but hopelessly unreliable machine. This triggered a retirement from frontline racing.

It returned to sports car racing in 1990 and made a Formula One engine for McLaren in 1994. This partnership lasted just one year and in six subsequent seasons with the Jordan and Prost teams, it failed to win a race. Peugeot withdrew from the sport at the end of the 2000 season.

Peugeot

Country of origin	France
Date of foundation	1889
Active years in Grands Prix	1895–1902 1906–14
Grand Prix victories	13

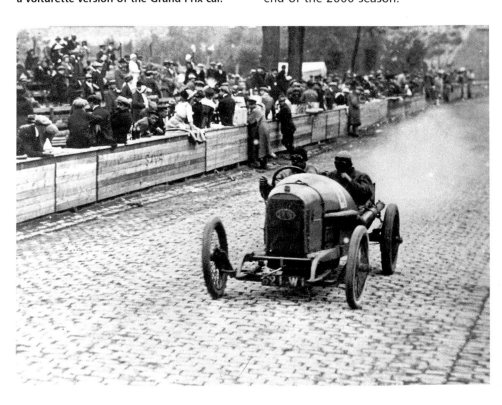

Renault

The son of a button manufacturer, Louis Renault first got into car manufacture after devising a successful improvement to the gearbox of his own de Dion car in the 1890s. Backed by his brothers Fernand and Marcel, he set up a factory to produce Renault cars. Louis and Marcel raced these machines in the early city-to-city events.

The brothers and the little Renaults were brilliant performers, often beating cars massively more powerful. But in the catastrophic 1903 Paris–Madrid race, Marcel was one of the fatalities. Louis finished second in that event, but retired from competitive driving thereafter. The newly inaugurated Grand Prix competition of 1906 led Renault back to the sport, producing a new car for Ferenc Szisz – formerly Louis's riding mechanic – to drive. He took it to victory. The company continued racing until 1908.

It returned, 69 years later, with a car that was to change the face of Formula One racing: the turbo-charged RS01. Jean-Pierre Jabouille's Renault took victory in the 1979 French Grand Prix, the first for the turbocharged engine, and before long the rest of the grid was forced to follow suit. After missing out on the 1983 World Championship,

▲ The winning car of the first ever Grand Prix was this Renault, driven by Ferenc Szisz.

Renault withdrew as a works team at the end of 1985, though it continued to supply engines to other teams.

This continued after the turbo era. In 1989, it debuted its V10 engine with the Williams team. This configuration was as widely copied as the earlier turbo. Renault V10s powered Williams and Benetton to five World Drivers' titles between 1992 and 1997, after which it withdrew once more. It returned as a works team in 2002, having bought out the Benetton team. Fernando Alonso's victory in the 2003 Hungarian Grand Prix marked a return to winning ways.

Renault	
Country of origin	France
Date of foundation	1898
Active years in Grands Prix	1901–08, 1977–85 2002–present
Grand Prix victories	16 (+ 2 pre-championship)

▼ Jarno Trulli in the Renault R202 retired from the 2002 Malaysian Grand Prix. The team had re-entered Formula One that season.

Sunbeam

▼ Jean Porporato in a Sunbeam at Indianapolis in 1915. He qualified in sixth position but retired with piston failure.

Victory in France in 1923 made Sunbeam the first British constructor to win a Grand Prix.

First and foremost a production car company, its technical director Louis Coatalen was a big believer in racing and took the company into voiturette ("small car") competition in 1910. With third, fourth and fifth places overall, Sunbeams took the first three places in the voiturette class of the 1912 French Grand Prix. The class victory was repeated a year later.

Coatalen recruited former Peugeot designer Ernest Henry to produce a Grand Prix car for the new 2-litre formula of 1922. It proved ineffective against the new Fiats, leading to

Sunbeam

Country of origin	United Kingdom
Date of foundation	1904
Active years in Grands Prix	1911–26
Grand Prix victories	3 pre-championship

Henry's replacement by one of the Fiat's designers Vincent Bertarione. For 1923, the Italian produced a car so similar to the 1922 Fiat that it was instantly dubbed "the green Fiat". It proved very effective and enabled Henry Segrave to come through for victory in France – ironically after the faster, newly-supercharged Fiats had retired when dominating.

For 1924, Sunbeam development engineer Captain Jack Irving devised Sunbeam's own supercharger, and in compressing the fuel/air mixture rather than merely the air, it allowed for lower internal temperatures and therefore more power. So equipped, the 1924 Sunbeam dominated the French Grand Prix from the start but retired with electrical trouble.

Soon afterwards, poor financial performance forced the termination of the company's racing programme, though it was later successful in securing world speed records.

▼ Henry Segrave in the Sunbeam 2-litre at the French Grand Prix in 1925.

Tyrrell

▼ Jackie Stewart gives the Tyrrell its first Grand Prix outing in 1970 at Canada. He would win the 1971 title with the car.

Ken Tyrrell was a timber merchant who had been moderately successful as a driver in the British Formula 500/Formula Three series in the 1950s. But he found his true vocation as a team entrant. In 1964, he teamed up with a promising young Scottish driver, Jackie Stewart, and together they stormed to victory in the British Formula Three Championship.

Stewart immediately graduated to Formula One, leaving Tyrrell to find further success as an entrant in Touring Car and Formula Two racing. Stewart continued to drive for Tyrrell in between his Formula One commitments, and for 1968 the pair were reunited properly in Formula One. Tyrrell had arranged that he be provided with a Matra chassis in which he would install the Ford Cosworth DFV engine. With Stewart driving, the team were close runners-up in the World Championship that year. Still with a Matra-Ford they went one better in 1969, dominating the season.

The Matra association then ended, and after purchasing a March for 1970 as a stop-gap, the first "Tyrrell" car appeared at the end of that season. Designed by Derek Gardner, the chassis had clear Matra influences. Powered by the ubiquitous Ford Cosworth DFV, it dominated the 1971 season as Stewart took his second world title. Tyrrell took the corresponding constructors' title in its first full season of racing.

The team remained a major force for the remaining two years of Stewart's career, but Jackie retired from the sport after securing title number three in 1973. Stewart's intended replacement, François Cevert, was killed practising for what was due to be Stewart's final race, a body blow to the team. Tyrrell instead recruited Formula One new boys Jody Scheckter and Patrick Depailler and enjoyed some success, but the glory days of Stewart were over.

A six-wheeler in 1976 gave the team lots of publicity as well as a 1-2 at the Swedish Grand Prix, but it was never repeated. The four-wheel replacement, the 008, won the 1978 Monaco Grand Prix with Depailler, but the team was struggling to generate commercial backing as Formula One entered a

▲ Jody Scheckter leads second-placed team-mate Patrick Depailler to take the first and only victory for a six-wheeled car.

▼ Jean Alesi – here in the 1990 Mexican Grand Prix – gave the team its last strong year. He scored second at Phoenix.

Tyrrell	
Country of origin	United Kingdom
Date of foundation	1970
Active years in Grands Prix	1970–98
Grand Prix victories	23 (+ 1 Constructors' Cup)

slicker, more expensive age. There were some bright spots – Michele Alboreto won a couple of races in the early 1980s, and Jean Alesi showed that the 1990 Tyrrell 019 was perhaps the best chassis on the grid – but overall the trend was downward.

The team was bought out at the end of 1997 by British American Tobacco. Ken Tyrrell died in 2001, aged 77, and the Formula One world mourned one of the last direct links to an earlier era.

Vanwall

Vanwall won the inaugural Formula One World Constructors' Championship in 1958, and so achieved the ambition of its founder Tony Vandervell, the British industrialist who had vowed to one day beat Ferrari.

Vandervell was the proprietor of Vandervell Bearings, whose patented "thinwall" bearing had been a major breakthrough for several manufacturers – including Ferrari – in making their engines more efficient. Vandervell had originally been part of the BRM trust, but left in frustration at the "management by committee" of that team in its early days. Instead, he persuaded Enzo Ferrari to sell him a series of Formula One cars that were then modified and raced as "Thinwall Specials".

The natural progression from this was a fully Vandervell car. This first appeared in 1955 and was labelled the "Vanwall". In place of the Ferrari engine was a four-cylinder unit derived from the single-cylinder Norton motorcycle race engines. Vandervell later commissioned de Havilland aerodynamicist Frank Costin to design a highly advanced low-drag body for it. Costin, in turn, suggested that Vandervell commission Lotus' Colin Chapman to make modifications to

▼ 1958 Vanwall Formula One car. Its sleek aeronautic-inspired lines helped make it the quickest car in a straight line.

Vanwall	
Country of origin	United Kingdom
Date of foundation	1955
Active years in Grands Prix	1955–58
Grand Prix victories	9 (+ 1 Constructors' Cup)

▼ Tony Vandervell (*left*) with mechanics at Pescara, Italy, in 1957.

the chassis and suspension. The combined result of all this development was that the Vanwall was the fastest car of 1957, and Tony Brooks and Stirling Moss gave it its first victory in the British Grand Prix of that year.

Brooks and Moss won six Grands Prix for the team in 1958, ensuring the Constructors' title. But in the final race of the season, at Morocco, third team driver Stuart Lewis-Evans crashed and received fatal burns. Vandervell, in failing health anyway, was devastated by the loss of his driver and he announced his retirement from the sport. The team did struggle on for another couple of seasons, appearing sporadically, but the serious challenge was over. Vandervell died in 1967.

▲ Stirling Moss and Tony Brooks in 1957. These two gifted drivers ensured Vanwall's first Grand Prix win at Aintree that year.

Williams

▼ Alan Jones in the Williams FW06 ran a sensational race at Long Beach in 1978, to firmly establish the team for the first time.

Frank Williams founded the team that came to dominate Formula One for much of the 1980s and 1990s in 1977. A keystone to its success was his chief designer Patrick Head.

Prior to this, Williams had eked out an existence on the fringes of Formula One, grabbing the occasional result but being perpetually underfunded. With the Head-designed Williams FW06 of 1978, the team's form enabled it to attract decent backing. The follow-up FW07 of 1979 gave the team its first victory, at the British Grand Prix, with Clay Regazzoni. Team-mate Alan Jones went on to dominate the second half of the season before giving the team its first World Championship in 1980.

Williams driver Keke Rosberg took the last ever DFV-powered World Championship in 1982. From the end of 1983, Williams went into partnership with Honda, a combination that yielded World Constructors' Championships in 1986 and 1987; Williams driver Nelson Piquet took the World Champion title in the latter year. After being surprisingly

dropped by Honda, Williams took up with Renault, and this led to an even more dominant spell. A Williams-Renault driver was Champion in 1992, 1993, 1996 and 1997.

Since 2000, BMW has been the team's engine partner, and together they have been winning races on a regular basis since 2001.

◀ Nelson Piquet leads Nigel Mansell as the two Williams fight over victory in the 1987 British Grand Prix. Mansell won.

▼ Juan Pablo Montoya tests the BMW Williams FW24 on an artificially wet track at Valencia, Spain, in 2002.

Williams

Country of origin	United Kingdom
Date of foundation	1977
Active years in Grands Prix	1977–present
Grand Prix victories	112 (+9 Constructors' Cups)

Constructors: The Current Challengers

Today's Formula One grid comprises ten teams. Five of these – Ferrari, Jordan, McLaren, Renault and Williams – have winning pedigrees. The remaining five aspire to join their ranks. These are the challengers.

◀ Minardi at the German Grand Prix, 2003.

▼ Sauber at the Hungarian Grand Prix, 2003.

Ready for Battle

In recent years, major road car producing manufacturers have entered Formula One, sometimes as engine suppliers, as in the case of Mercedes, BMW and Honda, and sometimes as fully formed teams, as with Jaguar, Renault and Toyota. Formula One has provided the manufacturers with a superbly effective global marketing platform.

At the same time, the level of financial investment they have brought to their Formula One programmes has increased the cost of competing for everyone. For those few teams not in partnership with one of the major manufacturers, these are very tough times indeed.

This was emphasized at the beginning of both 2001 and 2002, when the Prost and Arrows teams respectively went out of business. The three remaining teams not aligned to manufacturers – Jordan, Minardi and Sauber – are striving to be the Davids to the manufacturers' Goliaths.

The team names at the forefront of Formula One – Ferrari, McLaren and Williams – have been the same for some time, and joining their winning circle is not easy. But, in 2003, Renault showed that it could be done, breaking back into that elite group by taking its first victory in 20 years. Toyota is fancied as the next manufacturer to make that breakthrough.

The challenger teams in action in 2003: *(from top)* Jaguar, BAR-Honda, Minardi, *(left)* Sauber, *(right)* Toyota.

BAR

Guided by Craig Pollock, the manager of 1997 World Champion Jacques Villeneuve, the tobacco giant British American Tobacco decided to create its own Formula One team. To this end it bought out the Tyrrell team and renamed it British American Racing, shortened to BAR.

The team was formed around Villeneuve, who drove the first BAR car in the 1999 Australian Grand Prix. It proved a difficult debut season as the team failed to score a single point.

With newly-acquired Honda works engines it improved during 2000, and Villeneuve scored a series of points finishes. Pollock resigned at the end of 2001 and was replaced by David Richards, whose Prodrive company has taken rallying World Championships with Subaru. Completing the new-broom era, original driver Villeneuve was replaced for 2004 by the Honda-favoured Takuma Sato.

BAR

Country of origin	United Kingdom
Date of foundation	1999
Active years in Grands Prix	1999–present
Grand Prix victories	0

▼ Olivier Panis driving the BAR-Honda 004 at the Canadian Grand Prix, Montreal, Canada, in 2002.

▲ (top) Jacques Villeneuve at the Spanish Grand Prix, Barcelona, in 1999. The team suffered a dismal first year.

▲ (above) Jacques Villeneuve drove the BAR Honda 003 to third place in Barcelona in 2001. It was the team's first podium.

Jaguar

▼ Eddie Irvine drove superbly to finish third in the 2001 Monaco Grand Prix, securing the first podium for the team.

Jaguar is the Formula One challenge of the Ford Motor Company. Still a young team, it has suffered a difficult gestation since its arrival in 2000.

Initially, Ford went into partnership with former World Champion Jackie Stewart, whose team Stewart Grand Prix won the 1999 European Grand Prix with Johnny Herbert. But Ford bought Stewart out in that year, wishing to own the team outright and re-brand it after its luxury car brand.

Several changes of management have characterized its efforts so far but results have been slow to come. Niki Lauda was replaced as boss pre-season 2003, but Mark Webber has since shown that progress has been made.

Jaguar

Country of origin	United Kingdom
Date of foundation	2000
Active years in Grands Prix	2000–present
Grand Prix victories	0

◄ Eddie Irvine acknowledges the plaudits for his third place at Monaco 2001. He equalled this result at Monza in 2002, but these were the highlights of three years' effort for the team.

▼ Spaniard Pedro de la Rosa pushes hard in the Jaguar R3 during the Austrian Grand Prix in 2002.

Minardi

Italy's "other" Formula One team after Ferrari, Minardi, has been part of the sport since 1985, when Formula Two constructor Giancarlo Minardi graduated to the upper echelon.

It has been a struggle for the tiny, underfunded team, but in the USA in 1990, Pierluigi Martini did give Minardi a front row qualifying position. He also scored the team's best-ever result with fourth place in the Portuguese Grand Prix in 1991.

Team founder Minardi sold his majority shareholding in the 1990s to Gabriele Rumi, who in turn sold out to airline boss Paul Stoddard in 2001. The team's plucky fight against the odds has won it many fans.

Minardi

Country of origin	Italy
Date of foundation	1985
Active years in Grands Prix	1985–present
Grand Prix victories	0

▲ Pierluigi Martini – Minardi's most successful driver – leads Stefan Bellof's Tyrrell in the 1985 Dutch Grand Prix.

▼ Mark Webber in the Minardi Asiatech PS02 during practice for the Austrian Grand Prix at the A1-Ring in 2002.

Sauber

 fter a successful campaign in sports cars that included World Championships and victory in the Le Mans 24 Hours, the Swiss-based Sauber team graduated to Formula One in partnership with Mercedes in 1993.

The Mercedes link came to an end in 1995. After a similarly short partnership with Ford, Sauber has found a level of stability using customer Ferrari engines since 1998.

Since that time the team has steadily improved its competitiveness to the point that it finished fourth in the World Constructors' Championship of 2001, ahead of many teams with factory engine partnerships.

With Kimi Raikkonen in 2001 and Felipe Massa in 2002, team boss Peter Sauber has earned a reputation as a talent scout. Both drivers had highly impressive Grand Prix seasons with Sauber as Formula One rookies. When McLaren bought out Raikkonen's Sauber contract for 2002, it gave the team a significant boost in budget.

▲ *(top)* Sauber versus Sauber. Jean Alesi and Johnny Herbert tangle at the Argentine Grand Prix, Buenos Aires, in 1998.

▲ *(above)* J.J. Lehto in the Sauber-Mercedes C12 at the Italian Grand Prix, Monza, in 1993. The team was in partnership with Mercedes during its first season of Formula One.

◄ Nick Heidfeld qualified only 17th in the 2002 Monaco Grand Prix, but he had helped to take the Sauber team to fourth place in the previous year's title chase.

Sauber	
Country of origin	Switzerland
Date of foundation	1970
Active years in Grands Prix	1993–present
Grand Prix victories	0

Toyota

T he world's third biggest motor manufacturer entered Formula One for the first time in 2002. Bravely, it decided to do so on its own rather than in partnership with an existing specialist team. Having enjoyed great success in the sport of rallying, it used the same Cologne base to establish its Formula One operation, although the impetus comes very much from the parent company in Japan.

Chief designer Gustav Brunner – a veteran of several Formula One teams, including Ferrari – designed the TF102 chassis into which the all-new Toyota V10 engine was installed. The car created a good impression immediately, with straightline speed as good as that of the top teams. It was also uncannily reliable for a brand new design, with Mika Salo scoring World Championship points in two of its first three races.

The facilities and investment underlying Toyota's first Formula One season left few onlookers with any doubts that this would, in time, come to be a serious force in Formula One. A more competitive season followed in 2003 as the team built up its experience of this very exacting sport. The team poached Renault's technical director Mike Gascoyne at the end of the year.

▲ Mika Salo's Toyota TF102 finished sixth in the debut race for Toyota at the Australian Grand Prix, Melbourne, in 2002.

Toyota	
Country of origin	Japan
Date of foundation	2001
Active years in Grands Prix	2002–present
Grand Prix victories	0

▼ Both Toyota drivers Mika Salo and Allan McNish get involved in a first corner accident at Melbourne in 2002.

The Circuits

There are 17 battlegrounds in 15 countries and five continents on which the Formula One World Championship is fought. The demands of each track are very different, placing varying strains on both man and machine. But, like Formula One itself, the venues and tracks are constantly altering, evolving with the technology of the cars, circuit safety and the commercial packaging of the sport. It is this latter demand that is leading to a changing geography of the championship, as the sport spreads its tentacles to new countries. As from 2004, the series no longer visits Austria but instead will pay its first visit to Bahrain and China. In the longer-term future, countries such as India, Turkey and Dubai are expected to host Grands Prix, illustrating its global appeal.

Key to Circuits

	Direction of race
	Start grid
	Finishing line
10	Bend number
6　289	Gear engaged/ speed km/h
T2	Timing point

◀ The Hockenheim track in 2000.

Australia *Albert Park*

Australia hosted its first World Championship Grand Prix in 1985, around a street circuit in Adelaide. It was here in 1986 that Nigel Mansell suffered his famous 300km/h (190mph) tyre blow-out that lost him the World Championship. This circuit continued to host the event until 1995, but two years earlier Melbourne – which has traditionally been in competitive opposition with Adelaide – secured a deal with Formula One boss Bernie Ecclestone to host the Grand Prix from 1996. It is now the traditional season-opening race, where the form of the new cars and car/driver combinations is revealed for the first time, setting the tone of the season to come.

The track chosen for the Melbourne race was, like Adelaide, a street circuit, albeit one constructed around the roads of a public park in the seaside district of St Kilda. There had been motor racing at Albert Park in the 1950s, but only for national-level events.

There was some local opposition against the Grand Prix, but this has melted away since the event has proved such a prestigious commercial success for the city. Albert Park is now one of the most successful Grands Prix in terms of attendance and financial return for the city and its restaurants and hotels.

The circuit follows quite closely the outline of the park's boating lake. Its sequence of fast bends, punctuated by three tight corners demands a tricky aerodynamic compromise between straightline speed and downforce. Braking and traction are especially important here, though its smooth,

▲ *(top)* Second place finisher Juan Pablo Montoya fends off Michael Schumacher's winning Ferrari, having earlier passed his rival round the outside.

▲ *(above)* Montoya's Melbourne form in the Williams FW24 raised hopes of a strong season in 2002. It was not to be.

▲ Martin Brundle gets airbourne in his Jordan 196 after a first corner accident at the Australian Grand Prix, 1996.

◀ David Coulthard moves over to let Häkkinen through to win the Australian Grand Prix in 1998.

Waite	
Clark	Hill
Lauda	Ascari
Marina	5 260
5 251	6 284
5 276	2 125
3 161	13
7 8 9	12 15
2 106 6 10	T2 14
5 270 6	11 3 143
T1 6 294	2 83 16
5	T3
4 201 3 138	Stewart
4 204 2	Prost
3 4 1	
2 122 3	Jones
6 275 3 123 6 286	
Whiteford	
Brabham	

Albert Park

Circuit length	5.316km (3.303 miles)
Lap record	1 min 27.724 secs M. Schumacher 2003
Previous winners	2003 D. Coulthard 2002 M. Schumacher 2001 M. Schumacher

▼ Michael Schumacher's Ferrari F1-2001 races past the Albert Park Marina in practice for the 2002 Australian Grand Prix.

dusty surface means that tyre wear tends to be low. This has ramifications on strategy, as it usually proves quicker over a race distance to pit only once, as the tyres degrade slowly.

On the fast approach to the tight first corner in the opening seconds of Melbourne's first Grand Prix in 1996, Martin Brundle's Jordan got airborne after clipping a rival's car. He barrel-rolled through the air in spectacular fashion but, remarkably, stepped out completely unhurt. A day earlier Jacques Villeneuve had made a great Formula One debut by qualifying his Williams on pole position.

There was controversy in 1998 when, after mishearing an instruction on the radio, McLaren's Mika Häkkinen pitted from the lead when the team were not ready for him. His delay allowed team-mate David Coulthard to take over at the front, but Coulthard then acceded to a team request that he back off and allow Häkkinen back in front.

Tragically, a track marshal was killed in 2001 after being hit by a wheel from Jacques Villeneuve's crashing BAR. Improvements to the protective fencing were made in time for the 2002 event. Michael Schumacher won this race for Ferrari after a thrilling early battle with Juan Pablo Montoya. Australia's Mark Webber made a great Grand Prix debut by bringing his Minardi home in fifth place in front of a crowd of adoring countrymen.

Austria *A1-ring*

◀ Jacques Villeneuve's Williams leads Eddie Irvine for Ferrari and David Coulthard for McLaren in 1997.

▼ Barrichello (*right*), after leading all the way, controversially moved aside for Schumacher on the line in 2002.

T he rapid success of Austrian driver Jochen Rindt in the early 1960s created such a whirlwind of interest that it sparked a campaign to have an Austrian Grand Prix as part of the World Championship.

Austria's only race venue at the time was in rural Zeltweg, where two runways of a still-used military airfield, nestling within a valley of the Styrian mountains, formed a temporary circuit. The first races were held there in 1958. Later, Rindt's sensational success in Formula Two – where as a novice he beat established Formula One stars such as Graham Hill – gained Zeltweg a World Championship Grand Prix for 1964. It was at this race that Rindt made his Formula One debut, although the event was won by Lorenzo Bandini's Ferrari after more favoured runners such as Jim Clark, Graham Hill and John Surtees retired with suspensions broken on the airfield's appallingly rough surface.

The governing body demanded changes to the track if the race were to continue as a championship event, but its continued use as an airfield made this impractical. Rindt's success helped raise finance for a circuit to be built on the other side of the valley, near the village of Spielberg. It was named the Osterreichring and opened in July 1969.

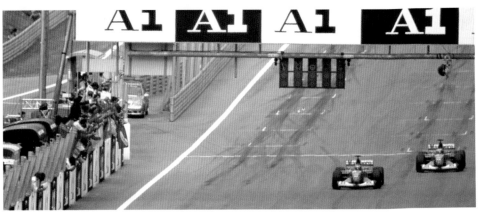

▼ Allan McNish's Toyota set against the Tyrolean backdrop in 2002. The track's sharp contours can be seen clearly.

It was a magnificent racing circuit, following the varying contours of the land through beautiful forests, with a sequence of supremely challenging fast bends. It held its first Grand Prix in 1970 and, fittingly, Rindt arrived there as the runaway leader of the championship. He retired from the race and, a few weeks later, was killed while practising for the Italian Grand Prix. The Austrian Grand Prix and the Osterreichring nonetheless continued to prosper, even more so after another Austrian driver – Niki Lauda – began to be successful.

The event was part of the calendar until 1987. In that year, television schedules were badly disrupted after it took three attempts to get the race underway, following a series of startline collisions on the narrow grid. At a time when there were already increasing safety concerns about the lack of run-off areas, it led to the race being dropped from the calendar once again. After some years, a new group of businessmen took over the circuit and,

Gosser Kurve

Jochen Rindt Kurve

Niki Lauda Kurve

Remus Kurve

A1 Kurve

Pit Lane

Power Horse Kurve

Castrol Kurve

A1-ring	
Circuit length	4.326km (2.688 miles)
Lap record	1 min 08.337 secs M. Schumacher 2003
Previous winners	2003 M. Schumacher 2002 M. Schumacher 2001 D. Coulthard

backed by the national telephone company A1, built a new, shorter track that incorporated much of the old Osterreichring but met modern safety standards. Named the A1-ring, it hosted its first Grand Prix in 1997.

One of the shortest tracks on the calendar, the A1-ring features two longish straights, including a couple of steep uphill sections. Engines are on full throttle for 60 per cent of the lap, and reach peak revs in top gear at three parts of the track. Interspersed by tight corners, it places a premium on power, braking and traction. Similar lap times can be achieved using very different aerodynamic set ups, so varied are the track's demands. Its low-grip, smooth surface makes it easy on tyre wear, and this makes one-stop race strategies the most common choice.

There was controversy here in 2002. After leading for the entire race, Ferrari's

► Montoya's Williams-BMW and Michael Schumacher's Ferrari collide in the 2001 race while fighting for the lead.

Rubens Barrichello was instructed to let team leader Michael Schumacher past on the last lap. He did so and the crowd jeered Schumacher on the podium.

The circuit's contract ended in 2003 and was not renewed. The final race saw Michael Schumacher coming back from a pit lane fire to win. It was a fittingly dramatic end to the era.

► Giancarlo Fisichella's pole-winning Benetton leads the 1998 Austrian Grand Prix.

Belgium *Spa-Francorchamps*

There have been two circuits within this spectacular wooded Ardennes valley, the first of which hosted Grands Prix between 1925 and 1970. Thereafter, it was deemed too dangerous for Formula One. A second, shorter track was built using part of the original public road circuit but then veering into a specially constructed downhill section. This first hosted a Grand Prix in 1983, and has been used ever since.

What both circuits had in common was their incredibly challenging nature. The original featured flat-out sweeps that followed the dramatically changing contours of the valley through villages, within inches of stone walls, trees and houses through its 12.8km (8 mile) length. In the final Grand Prix there, Chris Amon set the fastest lap at an average 244.74km/h (152.08mph). It was also dangerous, and had a horrific record of fatalities. Jackie Stewart's accident there in the 1966 Belgian Grand Prix initiated his long-running Formula One safety campaign.

The 1983 track used the same downhill section of public road to begin the lap, leading into the dramatic Eau Rouge bend, still considered the greatest challenge of all by most

▲ **Two competitors pass under a bridge as residents of a local hotel watch the action.**

▼ **The Jordan team took its first victory in fine style with a 1-2 in the wet 1998 Belgian Grand Prix, with Damon Hill leading team-mate Ralf Schumacher.**

Formula One drivers. In a good car with a brave driver, this left-right sweep, with a downhill approach and an uphill exit, can be taken foot-to-the-floor in top gear. A long, steep hill then leads to Les Combes, a tight second-gear right-hander, and the point where the new track parts with the old public road. A series of daunting, downhill bends takes the track to the valley's floor, where it rejoins the tail-end of the old circuit at Stavelot. A flat-out kink and short straight precede the "Bus Stop" chicane, so called because of its extreme tightness. The exit of this leads to La Source hairpin and the beginning of another lap.

The altitude variations and large area of forest lead to highly changeable weather conditions, and sudden heavy rain is always a possibility. Frequently, it can be raining on one side of the circuit and dry on the other.

One of the most dramatic Grands Prix of the modern era took place in 2000, with a wheel-to-wheel battle between title rivals Michael Schumacher and Mika Häkkinen. Schumacher had made a remarkable Formula One debut here in 1991 and, with four victories, had a special affinity with the place. For the 2000 race he had gambled on there being rain, and had set up his car with lots of downforce. But the rain held off,

Blanchimont

Bus Stop

Pit Lane

Stavelot

La Source

15

Fagnes

T2

14   13

Malmédy

Les Combes

Kemmel

Pouhon

Raidillon

Eau Rouge

Spa-Francorchamps

Circuit length	6.947km (4.317 miles)
Lap record	1 min 47.176 secs M. Schumacher 2002
Previous winners	2002 M. Schumacher 2001 M. Schumacher 2000 M. Häkkinen

▶ **Schumacher on three wheels after colliding with David Coulthard at Spa in 1998.**

allowing Häkkinen to close down Schumacher's lead. Much quicker up the hill to Les Combes, Häkkinen moved to the Ferrari's inside but, at almost 320km/h (200mph), Schumacher edged the McLaren towards the grass, forcing Häkkinen to back off. The Finn was now angry. On the next lap, at exactly the same place, Schumacher and Häkkinen came up to lap the BAR of Ricardo Zonta. Schumacher passed him on the left, Häkkinen on the right. A startled Zonta watched in amazement as Häkkinen took the lead, on his way to a great gladiatorial victory.

A row over tobacco advertising saw Spa removed from the 2003 calendar, but its planned return for 2004 has brought a sigh of relief from aficionados of the sport.

▶ **Race winner Ayrton Senna leads McLaren team-mate Gerhard Berger in 1990.**

Brazil *Interlagos*

S ituated on shifting land between two underground lakes – hence its name – the Interlagos track first hosted local-level motor racing in the 1930s. Back then it was an open site within an unpopulated area south of the city of São Paulo. The subsequent population explosion of that city saw the site enveloped by shanty town *favellas*.

Nonetheless, with Emerson Fittipaldi giving Brazil her first World Champion in 1972, Interlagos hosted a round of the series the following year. In fairytale fashion, Fittipaldi won in his JPS Lotus, a feat he repeated the following year in a McLaren. In that race he could hear the screaming cheers of the crowd as he passed race leader, Ronnie Peterson. In 1975, another Brazilian, Carlos Pace, won the race for Brabham. It was to be his only Formula One victory before being killed in a plane crash two years later. The circuit was subsequently renamed in his memory.

The track used between 1973 and 1980 was wonderfully demanding, with a banked, almost flat-out first corner. Unusually, the track ran in an anti-clockwise direction. Concerns about lack of run-off areas for the ever-faster cars, and the intolerance of

ground-effect cars for the notoriously bumpy surface were the reasons given for moving the Brazilian Grand Prix to Rio de Janeiro in 1981, to a track that first hosted the race in 1978. Perhaps significantly, Brazil's new racing hero Nelson Piquet hailed from Rio.

But the later success of São Paulo's Ayrton Senna helped bring the impetus back to Interlagos. The mayor of the city struck a deal with Formula One supremo Bernie Ecclestone for the race to return there for 1990, on a new circuit within the same grounds.

Senna himself contributed to the design, which used some of the original

track but which by-passed the fast but dangerous former Turn One. The outer part of this track largely comprised part of the old circuit, and was very quick, with a fast uphill kink on to the pit straight. A downhill left-right S-bend (later named the Senna Esses) signalled the start of the new section, with an infield comprising mainly tight bends, though with one hugely challenging downhill fifth-gear left-hander, Turn 11.

Yet the bumps of the old track remained a problem, and no matter how much resurfacing work is done, new bumps always seem to appear. The shifting land beneath is the culprit,

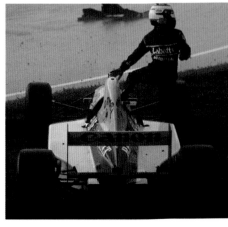

▲ *(top)* Nigel Mansell got his Ferrari career off to a great start with a win at Brazil in 1989.

▲ *(above)* Alain Prost spun his Williams-Renault out of the lead in the 1993 event, handing victory to arch-rival Ayrton Senna.

◀ Race winner Ayrton Senna leads the field in the 1991 race; Mansell follows.

Pinheirinho

Arquibandcadas

Bico de Pato

Laranja

Subida do Boxes

Ferra Dura

Mergulho

Junçao

Pit Lane

T3

T2

T1

Senna Esses

Curva do Sol

Descida do Lago

Reta Oposta

◄ Local boy Carlos Pace won here in 1975. The track was later renamed in his honour.

▼ Race winner Michael Schumacher leads younger brother Ralf in the 2002 event.

Autodromo Carlos Pace

Circuit length	4.308km (2.677 miles)
Lap record	1 min 14.75 secs M. Schumacher 2000
Previous winners	2003 G. Fisichella 2002 M. Schumacher 2001 D. Coulthard

and it brings an extra dimension to the problems faced by drivers and engineers as they try to set up the cars. Ride heights have to be bigger than at any other track on the calendar, reducing the aerodynamic efficiency and grip of the cars. Furthermore, the changeable weather can wreak havoc – as was seen in 2003 when a huge storm 30 minutes before the start created conditions that caused a chaotic, accident-infested race.

In 2001, Juan Pablo Montoya, in only his third Grand Prix, made himself a hero to millions, when he took the lead from Michael Schumacher with a daring wheel-rubbing move at the end of the straight into the Senna Esses. He pulled away quickly, and looked set for victory, but was later hit by the lapped car of Jos Verstappen. Despite his Colombian nationality, Montoya is a favourite with the wildly enthusiastic Interlagos fans. São Paulo native, Rubens Barrichello, closely follows him in their affections.

Canada *Montreal*

Situated on the Ile Notre Dame, a man-made island between the St Lawrence River and the St Lawrence Seaway, the Montreal track first hosted the Canadian Grand Prix in 1978, after the old Mosport circuit was deemed too dangerous.

The island had been built to house the world trade fair of 1967, and it hosted the Olympic Games of 1976, but more usually was parkland. The park roads were joined to form a circuit of long, fast straights and tight chicanes and hairpins. The fans went home very happy after the 1978 race, when local hero Gilles Villeneuve won for the first time in his Ferrari.

Villeneuve featured heavily in 1979 too, finishing second after a thrilling lead battle with the faster Williams of Alan Jones. In the wet 1981 race, he finished third despite running for much of the distance with no front wing.

◄ Gilles Villeneuve celebrates his first Formula One win with Quebec Premier Pierre Trudeau, on the Montreal podium in 1978.

▼ Mika Häkkinen's McLaren leading a lapped Arrows at the hairpin during the 2000 event.

But the month before he was due to take part in the 1982 event, he was killed during qualifying for the Belgian Grand Prix. The circuit was renamed in his memory.

The 1982 race saw further tragedy when Ricardo Paletti was killed in a startline accident, when his Osella rammed into the back of the stalled pole position Ferrari of Villeneuve's former team-mate, Didier Pironi.

The circuit has changed little over the years, and it invariably produces an exciting race. The combination of high speeds on the long straights, followed by tight second-gear bends, means that it is the most punishing circuit of all for brakes. The carbon-fibre brake discs of

Droit du Casino

Pit Lane

Coin Senna

pingle

Pont de la Concorde

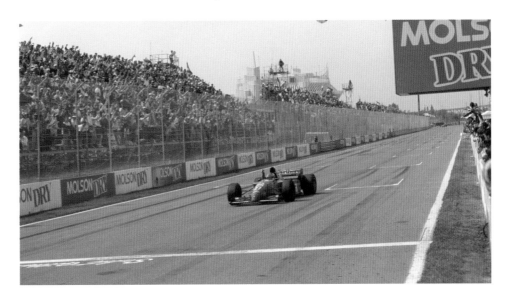

◀ Nelson Piquet's Benetton inherited a last-lap victory in 1991 after Mansell stalled his Williams while waving to the crowd.

Circuit Gilles Villeneuve

Circuit length	4.350km (2.703 miles)
Lap record	1 min 15.960 secs J. P. Montoya 2002
Previous winners	2003 M. Schumacher 2002 M. Schumacher 2001 R. Schumacher

modern Formula One cars begin to oxidize at temperatures over 600°C (1112°F). Here, they reach over 800°C (1472°F) repeatedly and are rarely allowed to drop below 500°C (932°F) before they are needed again. Brake wear is extreme, and lack of brakes is a frequent cause of retirement.

But it was the pressure of rival, Mika Häkkinen, rather than the lack of brakes that caused Michael Schumacher to crash out of the race in 1999. The two had engaged in a fierce duel that took them clear of the rest of the field. Finally, Michael took a little too much speed into the final corner and smashed hard into the unforgiving wall at its exit. Häkkinen duly took the win, a vital part of his successful campaign that year.

In 2001, the battle for victory was an all-Schumacher affair as Michael's Ferrari led early from brother Ralf's Williams-BMW. For lap after lap, Ralf would edge alongside in the final chicane, only to be discouraged as Michael veered toward him. The race's

turning point came when the Ferrari had to pit for fuel. Ralf's fuel tanks were bigger, and with little tyre wear from the dusty track, he was able to reel off four super-quick laps with clear air ahead of him. This enabled him to make his pitstop and rejoin the race in the lead for a comfortable victory.

Rows over tobacco advertising have threatened the future of this event (the 2004 event was initially cancelled) but its popularity with teams and fans has helped maintain its place on the calendar.

▼ Jean Alesi takes the flag for the only Formula One win of his career, in 1995.

Europe *Nürburgring*

The European Grand Prix used to be a title bestowed in turn on a different European race each year, but fell into disuse in the mid-1970s. It was revived in 1983, when Brands Hatch hosted a Grand Prix just a few months after Silverstone's British Grand Prix. The title was subsequently used to cover any doubling-up of races in the same country: the new Nürburgring held the European Grand Prix in 1984 (Hockenheim held the German Grand Prix); in 1985, Brands Hatch featured the European race, while Silverstone's event bore the "British" tag. Then, in 1993, Donington Park was granted a Grand Prix of Europe, and Silverstone retained its regular British Grand Prix slot on the Formula One calendar.

More recently, the popularity of Formula One in Germany, following the success of Michael Schumacher, has made it viable for that country to host two Grands Prix per season. One of them, that held at the Nürburgring, now holds the full-time claim to the European Grand Prix title.

The "new" Nürburgring was first used in 1984. It was built as a modern venue to attract Formula One back to

▲ An aerial view of the new Nürburgring. The new circuit was built because of serious safety concerns about the original track.

▼ Ralf Schumacher (*right*) fights out the first corner of the 2002 European Grand Prix with Williams-BMW team-mate Juan Pablo Montoya. Rubens Barrichello's Ferrari (*directly behind Montoya*) won the race.

the region after the original track – a 22.5km (14 mile) section of road running through forested valleys – was deemed too dangerous, following Niki Lauda's near-fatal accident in 1976.

It is a relatively flat and featureless circuit, with constant radius bends and plenty of run-off area. Its surface is quite abrasive, demanding a fairly hard tyre compound. After a series of first corner incidents – where out-of-control cars going through the gravel trap had a tendency to come back on to the track on the exit as other cars filed past – the layout was changed for 2002. A double bend now takes the racing line out of reach of first corner spinners.

One of the most exciting races of modern Formula One took place at this track in 1995. It began in wet but drying conditions. Most chose to start on wet tyres, but not Jean Alesi in the Ferrari. As David Coulthard's Williams led from Michael Schumacher's Benetton and Damon Hill's Williams, Alesi was able to use his fantastic car control to hang on to them.

As the track began to dry, so the wet-tyred leaders had to pit – leaving Alesi with a 20-second lead and no

Bit Kurve

Itt Curve

RTL Kurve

Veedol Schikane

Dunlop Kurve

Coca-cola Kurve

Ford Kurve

Pit Lane

Mercedes Schikane

need to stop. With Coulthard now second, Schumacher and Hill were engaged in a furious battle over third place, and the German gave the Brit a chop on one occasion that almost took the Williams off the circuit. Eventually Hill succeeded in getting by, but then threw away the move by getting off line at the next corner, allowing Schumacher to retake the place. Michael then began to pull away.

Coulthard began to suffer handling difficulties, and was passed by both Schumacher and Hill, but still Alesi was

leading comfortably, even after a routine refuelling stop. But Schumacher began his relentless chase of the Ferrari. Alesi and his team took a long time to wake up to the threat of the closing Benetton. By the time Jean tried to respond, it was too late; Schumacher was now on his tail. With seven laps to go, Schumacher made an aggressive move down the inside into the chicane. It gave Alesi the option of making way or taking them both off. He chose the former, allowing Schumacher his seventh win of the season, on his way to the world title.

Nürburgring	
Circuit length	5.144 km (3.196 miles)
Lap record	1 min 32.2265 secs M. Schumacher 2002
Previous winners	2003 R. Schumacher 2002 R. Barrichello 2001 M. Schumacher

▲ Johnny Herbert's Stewart took victory in the 1999 European Grand Prix.

▶ Jacques Villeneuve withstood pressure from Michael Schumacher to take his first Formula One win, at the Nürburgring, 1996.

▲ (top) Alain Prost's McLaren-Porsche won the first race held at the new Nürburgring for the 1984 European Grand Prix.

▲ (above) Niki Lauda's BRM in 1973: airborne action at the old Nürburgring.

France *Magny-Cours*

A race enthusiast farmer, Jean Bernigaud, built the original track on this site in 1960. Situated a few miles away from the town of Nevers, in the Loire Valley, it still nestles between green farmland and traditional French châteaux.

It was not until 1991 that the circuit played host to the French Grand Prix, by which time it was very different from the original. The current format was built in 1988, with the help of government grants. The Ligier team, later renamed Prost, was based here until Alain Prost moved it to Paris in 2000. Magny-Cours was also the base for the Winfield Racing School that established a whole generation of Elf-backed French racing drivers in the 1970s and 1980s. François Cevert, Patrick Depailler, Jacques Laffite and René Arnoux, among others, all started their careers here as raw novices. Laffite and Arnoux were consultants for the layout of the current track.

The most notable characteristic of this circuit is its incredibly smooth, bump-free surface. Teams can set the ride height of their cars lower here than at any other track, bringing big benefits in aerodynamic grip. Many of the corners are long and flowing, meaning the tyres are under lateral load for

◀ David Coulthard scythes down the inside of Michael Schumacher in 2000.

◀ Nigel Mansell (Williams) leads Alain Prost (Ferrari) in 1991.

▼ *(below left)* Ralf Schumacher's Williams-BMW leads brother Michael's Ferrari in 2001.

a long time. Combined with the soft compounds allowed by the surface, this makes tyre wear a critical factor.

The 1999 French Grand Prix at Magny-Cours was a fascinating struggle between several teams and drivers,

with changeable weather making the outcome uncertain right to the end.

The sky was threatening but the track dry as the race started, and Rubens Barrichello's Stewart led from pole position ahead of Jean Alesi's Sauber and David Coulthard's McLaren. At the end of the first lap, Heinz-Harald Frentzen's Jordan and Michael Schumacher's Ferrari followed in fourth and fifth place. Coulthard quickly passed both Alesi and Barrichello to take the lead. He pulled out a big gap over the rest before pulling to the side of the track with electrical failure on the 10th lap.

As Barrichello retook the lead, the rain began falling. But then stopped again after a couple of laps. Alesi was coming under pressure from Frentzen, and behind them was Mika Häkkinen, who had passed Schumacher. Häkkinen then passed Frentzen, Alesi and Barrichello in quick succession to take the lead in his McLaren.

On the 21st lap, the rain arrived properly, and everyone pitted for wet weather tyres. The Stewart team gave Barrichello a very quick stop, enabling

Imola

Nürburgring

Adelaide

Golf

T1

4 2.10

4

5

5 2.60

6

10

11

12

13

7

T2

5 2.45

4 2.10

9

2 80

4 185

3

8

5 2.60

1

2 80

2

2 2.65

4 2.00

14

5 2.45

ril

2.5 12.0

2 80

Pit Lane

16 15

2 1.36

T3

Château
d'Eau

Chicane

2 80

Grande Courbe

him to get out ahead of Häkkinen.
The heavens opened fully on lap 24,
and Alesi spun out on a deep puddle,
bringing Frentzen up to third. The rain
was now so heavy that the safety car
came out, neutralizing the race for the
next 11 laps. With the race back on,
Häkkinen attempted to wrest the lead
back from Barrichello but spun,
dropping to seventh. At around the
same time, Schumacher – who had lost
radio contact with his pit – had passed
Frentzen and was in now second place.

After one failed attempt, Schumacher
succeeded in passing Barrichello on lap
42. But soon after, he slowed due to
electrical glitches in his car. He came in
early for his second fuel stop to have
the problem attended to. Barrichello
thus led again but by now Häkkinen
was carving back through the field and,
after passing Frentzen, he took the lead
from Barrichello for a second time.
He began pulling away at the rate of
three seconds per lap. Häkkinen and
Barrichello made their second planned
fuel stops, putting Frentzen in front.

Frentzen's Jordan had bigger fuel
tanks than the other cars and, with the
slower pace forced by the rain and the
safety car, he now had enough fuel
in reserve not to make his originally
planned second stop. The McLaren and

Stewart teams waited for Frentzen to
come in – and waited, and waited.
At the end of 72 laps, Frentzen crossed
the line to give Jordan an unexpected
victory from Häkkinen and Barrichello.

Magny-Cours	
Circuit length	4.411km (2.741 miles)
Lap record	1 min 15.512 secs J. P. Montoya 2003
Previous winners	2003 R. Schumacher 2002 M. Schumacher 2001 M. Schumacher

▼ Schumacher leads into turn one at the
start of the French Grand Prix, 2 July 2000.

Germany *Hockenheim*

ockenheim has been the venue of the German Grand Prix since 1977 (with the exception of 1985, when the new Nürburgring hosted its second Grand Prix), though it hosted the event on one occasion before that, in 1970. For many years, it was the fastest Grand Prix track on the calendar, due to two very long straights. Even since being interrupted by chicanes in the 1980s, these stretches still allowed the Formula One cars of the 1990s to reach over 360km/h (224mph) in top gear. The straights – which ran through a wood – featured no spectating areas and were linked by a stadium section, where the crowds gather and where the pit lane is situated. This layout was used for the last time in 2001. For the 2002 race, a new section of track cut out much of the length of the straights, turning right through the former wood around half way down the first straight into a new infield section that then links back up with the truncated second straight just before the stadium. The new layout enables the cars to be seen by spectators for a greater proportion of the lap.

Situated around 112km (70 miles) south of Frankfurt, the original Hockenheim circuit was built as a test track by Mercedes in the late 1930s. When a new autobahn was built in the 1960s, it split the original track in two,

▲ *(top)* Jacky Ickx's Ferrari leads Jochen Rindt's Lotus in the first Grand Prix to be held at Hockenheim in 1970. Rindt won.

▲ *(above)* Niki Lauda on his way to an emotional Ferrari win in 1977.

▼ Jarno Trulli's Jordan leads Olivier Panis' BAR during a midfield battle in the last Grand Prix to be held on the unfettered Hockenheim track, in 2001.

but, using compensation money from the government, the circuit owners planned a new layout using only the far side of the former site. Racing began on this new track in 1966. Two years later, it gained notoriety when the great Jim Clark was killed here in a Formula Two race. His Lotus went out of control through a left-hand kink on the first straight, probably as the result of a slow puncture, and came to rest against a tree.

Safety standards were improved by the erection of barriers to protect cars from the trees. In 1970, under pressure from the Grand Prix Drivers' Association, the Nürburgring was being altered to improve safety, and so the German Grand Prix of that year was held at Hockenheim for the first time. The race was won by Jochen Rindt's Lotus. It would be another seven years before the event returned there, this time permanently, after the Nürburgring was finally dismissed as intrinsically too dangerous for Formula One. This had become clear through Niki Lauda's near-fatal accident there in 1976. It was therefore fitting that Lauda won the 1977 race at Hockenheim.

In 1980, Patrick Depailler was killed during a test session, when a suspected suspension failure put his Alfa Romeo head-on into the barriers at around 240km/h (150mph) at the Ost-Kurve. Another chicane was added to slow the cars through this section. Two years later, Didier Pironi's career came to an end after an accident caused by the

Hochgeschwindigkeits
(Parabalica) – Kurve

Einfahrt Parabalica

Spitzkehre

d-Kurve

Sachs-Kurve

Pit Lane

Sud-Kurve

Mobil 1 Kurve

Hockenheim	
Circuit length	4.574km (2.842 miles)
Lap record	1 min 14.917 secs J. P. Montoya 2003
Previous winners	2003 J. P. Montoya 2002 M. Schumacher 2001 R. Schumacher

appalling visibility in wet conditions. Spray on the fast straights tends to be slow in dispersing, hemmed in by trees.

But some drivers had a special affinity with the track, notably Gerhard Berger. He won here for Ferrari in 1994, his only victory in his three-year second stint with the team. He was on-course to win the event in 1996 for Benetton until his engine blew on the last lap, handing victory to Damon Hill. But his greatest race here was his last one, in 1997. He had missed the previous three races because of a sinus problem, and been replaced by stand-in Alex Wurz.

Unfortunately for Berger, Wurz had performed superbly, and questions were being asked about whether Berger was needed. But worse, much worse, in the days leading up to his comeback, Berger learned that his father had been killed in a plane crash. It was somehow fitting that Berger should dominate the weekend. He started from pole position and led the race from beginning to end. At the end of the season he retired.

▼ *(left)* **Michael Schumacher in the Ferrari 310B on his way to second place in 1997.**

▼ *(right)* **A Toyota TF102 approaches the new hairpin at the heavily remodelled Hockenheim track during the German Grand Prix in 2002.**

Great Britain *Silverstone*

In late-1940s Britain, the search was on for a major new race venue. Brooklands was no more, with half of its speed bowl destroyed to make room for aircraft production facilities. But as the war took away, so it created. In the heart of rural Northamptonshire, near the sleepy little village of Silverstone, there was a wartime airfield that was no longer needed. The perimeter roads of the runways made for a perfect high speed challenge. In 1948, it hosted the British Grand Prix. It has held it, on and off, ever since.

Initially, the country's governing body, the RAC, wished to spread its favours, and for a time the race alternated between Silverstone and Aintree near Liverpool. Subsequently – until 1986 – Brands Hatch in Kent took over the Aintree slot. But when Brands was deemed no longer suitable for Formula One, Silverstone monopolized the event.

It was a fast, flat and featureless track, very demanding and exacting, but for some drivers slightly disorienting. The early straw-bale markers soon gave way, first to oil drums, then concrete posts, and finally proper kerbs. But the farm remained in the track's infield – with the wheat usually high by the time

▲ *(top)* Jack Brabham took his Cooper to victory at Silverstone in 1960, on his way to a second World Championship.

▲ *(above)* Michael Schumacher (Ferrari) celebrates victory in the 2002 race at the same Silverstone venue at which he broke his leg in 1999.

of mid-July, the British Grand Prix slot – and the "Silverstone hare" still does invariably appear on-track during the weekend. Until the late 1980s, the layout remained much the same, once the original incorporation of the airfield runway was abandoned after 1948.

The corners were fast, and demanded a lot of commitment and precision on the way in. After Jody Scheckter crashed at the quick Woodcote corner, at the end of the first lap of the 1973 race, taking much of the field out with him, a chicane was incorporated there to slow things down. But it was still a fast track, and vied with the Osterreichring from the mid-1970s to mid-80s as the fastest on the calendar. In 1985, Keke Rosberg's turbocharged Williams-Honda set a qualifying lap speed of 258.97km/h (160.924mph), a Formula One record that stood until 2002.

This was rather too fast, in fact. The run-off areas demanded by these sort of speeds would have moved the spectators impossibly far back from the action. For the 1992 race, a complete redesign was in place. There was a new infield section before Woodcote, entered via the awesome Bridge Corner, a slightly banked top-gear right-hander. The right-left sweep of Becketts on to the Hangar Straight became more sharply defined, and there was a new section – Vale – between the Stowe and Club corners, which slowed things down further. Essentially, this remains the layout of the track today.

◄ Felippe Massa (Sauber) spinning at the first corner of the 2002 British Grand Prix.

Luffield
Priory
Bridge
Farm
Abbey
Club
Brooklands
Woodcote
Pit Lane
Copse
17
T3
16 15
T2
13 14
12
11
10
9
8
7
Stowe
Hanger Straight
Maggots
Becketts
Chapel
T1
6
5 4
3
2
1

But perhaps the most memorable Silverstone race of all time – and one of the greatest races in Formula One history – came on the old track, in 1987. The Williams-Hondas were the dominant machines of the time and no one other than their drivers, Nelson Piquet and Nigel Mansell, really had a chance. Piquet led the early going with Mansell chasing.

Then Mansell began to sense a vibration – a wheel weight had fallen off. It forced him to make an unplanned pit stop on lap 36 of the 65-lap race. With new tyres, he rejoined and with nothing to lose he turned up his turbo boost and set about catching his team-mate, now 28-seconds ahead.

He closed down at a rapid rate and the partisan crowd sensed something big was about to happen. With two laps to go, approaching Stowe corner at the end of the 305km/h (190mph) Hangar Straight, Mansell feigned for the outside. Piquet covered him and Mansell immediately darted to the inside and passed. Entering the last lap, Mansell's fuel read-out was telling him he had nothing left, but there was just enough to get him home. He ran out on the slowing down lap – and was mobbed.

Silverstone

Circuit length	5.141km (3.195 miles)
Lap record	1 min 22.236 secs R. Barrichello 2003
Previous winners	2003 R. Barrichello 2002 M. Schumacher 2001 M. Häkkinen

▼ *(left)* Ayrton Senna's McLaren leads Gerhard Berger's Ferrari in the 1988 race. Senna won; team-mate Prost withdrew.

▼ *(right)* Mansell-mania: the crowd invade the track after homegrown hero Nigel Mansell dominated the 1992 race in his Williams-Renault FW14B. Mansell's successes attracted a new breed of race fan to Silverstone.

Hungary *Hungaroring*

It was Formula One supremo Bernie Ecclestone who pushed hardest for a Grand Prix behind the old Iron Curtain. For several years there was talk of a Moscow Grand Prix, but discussions always broke down at an early stage. It was then suggested to Ecclestone that he look at Hungary, where the regime might be more accommodating.

There was already a history of motor racing in the country as it had hosted a pre-war Grand Prix around the streets of Budapest, and even as late as the 1960 the city had been host to other European touring car events. The government was sold on the idea of a Grand Prix but, after looking at feasibility studies, decided that a new purpose-built track should be created. Work began in 1985, ready for the inaugural Grand Prix of 1986. The circuit was to be built in a rural valley some miles outside the city. Situated in a natural amphitheatre, it allowed for superb viewing for spectators.

However, as the allocated land area was fairly small, the track had to turn in on itself several times. Consequently it is very tight, offering no real chance for the cars to stretch their legs and there is only one possible overtaking spot. In terms of the set-up required of the

▲ *(top)* Nigel Mansell pulls off after a rear wheel came adrift while he was leading the late stages of the 1987 race.

▲ *(above)* Damon Hill's Arrows passes Michael Schumacher's Ferrari to lead the 1997 race. He later hit trouble.

cars, it needs maximum wing settings, just like at Monaco. For 2003, a new section of track was built in an effort to encourage more overtaking.

Nelson Piquet won the first race on the new Hungarian track, in August 1986, in his Williams-Honda. He had earlier taken the lead with a stunning round-the-outside pass of Ayrton Senna's Lotus at the first corner, the Williams on full opposite lock as it completed the manoeuvre. Piquet won again the following year, but only after his team-mate Nigel Mansell's wheel nut came off while leading.

The 1989 race was perhaps the most exciting Hungarian race. After early-leader Riccardo Patrese retired

◀ Fernando Alonso won at the Hungaroring in 2003. At 22 years and 26 days he became the youngest ever Grand Prix winner.

Hungaroring

Circuit length	4.384km (2.724 miles)
Lap record	1 min 22.095 secs J. P. Montoya 2003
Previous winners	2003 F. Alonso 2002 R. Barrichello 2001 M. Schumacher

► **Mika Häkkinen (McLaren-Mercedes) took a dominant win at Hungary in 1999 in the absence of injured rival Michael Schumacher.**

his Williams with a punctured radiator, Ayrton Senna was leading in the McLaren and looked set for victory. But that was to reckon without Nigel Mansell, who had qualified his Ferrari in only 12th place. In the race his car was handling superbly, and he had quickly fought his way through the pack. He was on Senna's tail as they came up to lap the Onyx of Stefan Johansson, who kept well over to the left of the track, aware that the leaders were bearing down on him. Senna seemed caught momentarily off-guard and boxed himself in behind. Mansell, anticipating this superbly, swung across the back of Senna's gearbox with just millimetres to spare and passed both cars in one move, on his way to victory. It gave the lie to the track's no-passing reputation.

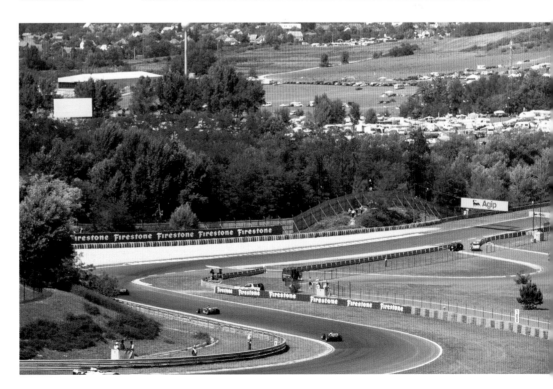

► **The scenic Hungaroring in August 2000.**

Italy *Monza*

S ituated in a former royal park in suburbs around 24km (15 miles) north of Milan, Monza is the oldest track on which the World Championship is still fought. It held its first Grand Prix in September 1922, and has hosted it almost every year since.

Monza was not the first purpose-built racing circuit in Europe – that honour belonged to Brooklands in Britain – but it was the first to be used for a Grand Prix. The 1922 Italian race, in fact, marked the first time that spectators were charged an entrance fee to watch a Grand Prix.

Comprising two circuits in one, the "speed bowl" was in essence an American-style oval track, with two long straights joined by two heavily banked corners. Within this was a "road circuit" designed to replicate the demands of public road racing that had comprised Grands Prix up until this time. The two tracks criss-crossed one another via a bridge, and shared the same pit straight. The speed bowl was demolished in 1938, but part of the banking was incorporated into the road course. In 1955, a new banked circuit was built to replace the pre-war one, and the layout allowed for a combination of banked and road circuit to be used. This combined track hosted the Grands Prix of 1955 and 1956, but

▲ *(top)* **The closest finish. Only 0.1seconds separated the first five finishers in the 1971 race. Peter Gethin got the verdict, from Peterson, Cevert, Hailwood and Ganley.**

▲ *(above)* **The first lap crash which claimed the life of Ronnie Peterson at the Italian Grand Prix on 10 September 1978.**

there were concerns about the stresses tyres and suspensions were subject to by the banking, and from 1957 the road course was reverted to once more. Even this was an extremely fast track, with much flat-out running and high speed bends, such as the Lesmos and Parabolica, making the races fantastically gripping slip-streaming battles where, typically, the outcome would be in doubt right up to the finish line.

There was one last Grand Prix held on the banking in 1960, but subsequently that section fell into disuse – though it still remains, an impressive weed-infested monument to a bygone era.

The high speeds meant the Monza circuit bore witness to many tragedies, and, initially, poor spectator protection meant they, too, were often involved. In 1928, Emilio Materassi crashed into the spectator enclosure on the main straight, killing 27 people and himself. As late as 1961, the Ferrari of Wolfgang von Trips reared along the spectator

◄ **The safety car leads the cars past the old banked circuit at the Italian Grand Prix in 2000.**

Curva del Vialane

Variante Ascari

Curva del Serraglio

Curva di Lesmos

Variante della Roggia

Curva Grande

Rettifilo Tribune

Pit Lane

Curva Parabolica

fencing approaching Parabolica before crashing back onto the track. He was killed, as were 14 spectators. Jochen Rindt lost his life here during practice for the 1970 race, and Ronnie Peterson died as a result of a first-lap start-line crash in the 1978 event.

Amid the fanatical Ferrari fans, Peter Gethin won for BRM in 1971, and his average speed of 242.62km/h (150.76mph) still stands as the fastest Grand Prix race average of all time. Subsequently, chicanes were installed to slow the cars down, and whilst making it safer it also brought about the end of the classic slipstreaming battles.

Monza	
Circuit length	5.793km (3.600 miles)
Lap record	1 min 21.832 secs M. Schumacher 2003
Previous winners	2003 M. Schumacher 2002 R. Barrichello 2001 J. P. Montoya

Winning the 2000 race helped Michael Schumacher on his way to reclaiming the title for Ferrari after 21 years. It also marked Schumacher's 41st Grand Prix victory, which brought him level to the record of Ayrton Senna. Schumacher – who had been racing against Senna at Imola in 1994, when the Brazilian crashed to his death – broke down in tears in the press conference.

▼ *(below)* Schumacher wins in 2000.

▼ *(bottom)* Italian fans celebrate the World Championship title won by Ferrari in 2001.

◄ *Tifosi* shout for Scuderia Ferrari at the Italian Grand Prix in 2001.

Japan *Suzuka*

osting the Japanese Grand Prix since 1987, Suzuka is renowned as one of the greatest challenges an Formula One driver can face. Its sequence of super-fast bends demand ultimate commitment and many rank its 290km/h (180mph) corner, 130R, as the ultimate test of nerve and skill.

Owned by Japanese manufacturer Honda, the circuit was built as a test track by the company in the early 1960s. Subsequent races were held there, though the newly-inaugurated but short-lived Japanese Grand Prix of 1976 and 1977 ran at the rival Fuji track.

It was not until the time of Honda's prominence as a Formula One engine supplier, in the mid-1980s, that it was able to exert its influence and have a Japanese Grand Prix reinstated to the calendar, this time at Suzuka.

As the Japanese race has usually been either the penultimate or final race of the year, it has frequently been host to championship deciders. In 1989, title rivals Alain Prost and Ayrton Senna collided at the chicane. Prost retired but Senna rejoined from the escape road and went on to win the race. He was then disqualified for rejoining the track

▲ Gerhard Berger took his first Ferrari win at Suzuka, 1987, with the F1/87. It was Formula One's fastest car by the end of the year.

in a dangerous manner, leaving him unable to overhaul Prost's points advantage in the one race remaining. A year later, Senna took his revenge as he again fought out the destiny of the crown with Prost. Using his points advantage in his favour, as Prost had done the previous year, Senna simply drove his rival off the track at the first corner. Both retired into the gravel trap,

▼ Mika Häkkinen leads Michael Schumacher in the 2000 Japanese Grand Prix, as they fight for the World Championship title.

but Senna became World Champion. In 2000, Michael Schumacher clinched the first World Championship for a Ferrari driver in 21 years after a supremely tense battle with his only rival, McLaren's Mika Häkkinen. The Finn led the first part of the race, with Schumacher following in his tracks as both pulled well clear of the rest of the field. The McLaren was the first to make

Crossover

Spoon Curve

Degner Curve

Dunlop Curve

"S" Curves

T2

T1

First Curve

Pit Lane

Hairpin Curve

Casio Triangle

Suzuka

Circuit length	5.859km (3.641 miles)
Lap record	1 min 33.408 secs R. Schumacher 2003
Previous winners	2003 R. Barrichello 2002 M. Schumacher 2001 M. Schumacher

▶ Damon Hill took a superb victory in the 1994 Japanese Grand Prix. Rival Michael Schumacher got stuck behind Mika Häkkinen, losing vital time.

its routine fuel and tyre stop, but just as Häkkinen was rejoining, spots of rain began to fall. Critically, this meant Häkkinen was unable to generate sufficient heat into his new tyres and, for a couple of laps, he was slow. Schumacher, yet to stop and on tyres already up to temperature, was able to lap quickly enough to build sufficient gap to allow him to pit and rejoin without losing the lead. Häkkinen gave chase, but it was to no avail. In bringing the world title back to Italy, Schumacher had succeeded in doing what no one had managed since Jody Scheckter in 1979.

▶ Michael Schumacher sealed a record-breaking sixth World Championship title in Japan at the final round of the 2003 world championship series.

Malaysia *Sepang*

The Malaysian government sought to host a globally prestigious annual event as part of its programme of economic expansion, and Formula One fitted the bill perfectly. To this end, a brand new circuit was constructed on the outskirts of Kuala Lumpur, with facilities that rendered other Formula One venues previous-generation. It hosted its first Grand Prix in 1999.

The track is situated on a former stretch of derelict land adjacent to Kuala Lumpur airport. It was designed by German Hermann Tilke to incorporate a wide variation of corners. Two 0.9km (0.56-mile) straights are joined by a hairpin, but perhaps the most spectacular part of the track is an unusually wide and gradual chicane, where the Formula One cars sweep left-right at around 200km/h (125mph). Further around the lap, Turn 12 is a highly dramatic fourth gear downhill left-hander, leading into the loop that takes the cars down the first of the long straights.

Grand Prix spectators are housed in grandstands beneath spectacular sun-sensitive leaf-design roofing, with blinds that open and close according to the light. From there they can see much of the circuit, thanks to the land's contours and the site's relatively compact area.

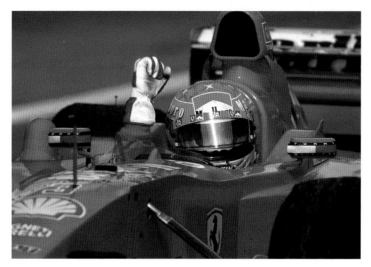

▲ Eddie Irvine was helped to victory by second-placed team-mate Michael Schumacher in 1999.

◄ Schumacher drove his Ferrari F1-2000 to victory at Sepang in 2000.

The inaugural race, the penultimate round of the 1999 championship, got the event off to a great start. Michael Schumacher, after breaking his leg at Silverstone, had missed much of the season, leaving his Ferrari team-mate Eddie Irvine to battle McLaren's Mika Häkkinen for the championship. Schumacher was finally fit to race again for Malaysia, and his brief was to aid Irvine in the Championship fight.

After setting pole position by over a second, Schumacher took off into the lead ahead of Irvine, whom he allowed past after four laps. As Irvine pushed on, intent on building up his lead, Schumacher endeavoured to slow the

◄ Alex Yoong (Minardi PS02) in his home Grand Prix was meant to pack the Sepang grandstands in 2002.

Pit Lane

4	260
2	85
6	303
2	114
3	176
2	124
4	258
4	210
5	267
6	290
2	106
4	255
2	103
4	174
4	244
4	193
4	200

McLarens behind him. David Coulthard found a chink in the defence, however. He barged past Schumacher and set off after Irvine, but on lap 15, Coulthard's car lost its fuel pressure and retired.

As Schumacher repeatedly prevented Häkkinen from making progress, Irvine built up enough of a lead that he was comfortably back in front after all had made their first fuel stops. Irvine then did a short second stint, increasing his lead even further, before a second and final fuel stop. He rejoined just behind Häkkinen, who then made his second stop. This left Schumacher – who wasn't making a second stop – in the lead from Irvine. Schumacher allowed Irvine through for a second time, and the Ferraris finished 1-2, with Häkkinen a frustrated third, allowing the title fight to go to the final round in Japan. It was a superb demonstration of team work from the Italian team.

Post-race, it was announced that the aerodynamic barge boards on the side of the Ferraris were of a shape not permitted by the regulations. They were initially disqualified, but reinstated on appeal a few days later.

▼ **The beautiful Malaysian paddock by night, illuminated by lasers.**

Sepang

Circuit length	5.542km (3.444 miles)
Lap record	1 min 36.412 secs M. Schumacher 2003
Previous winners	2003 K. Raikkonen 2002 R. Schumacher 2001 M. Schumacher

Monaco *Monte Carlo*

T he race around the streets of the tiny principality, home of the jet-set crowd and super-rich, has become synonymous with the image of Grand Prix racing. Since 1929, cars have raced past the yachts in the Mediterranean harbour, around tortuous bends more usually clogged with traffic. The slowest Grand Prix track on the calendar, it is also the most exacting. Unlike other tracks, there are no run-off areas and no margin for error. One slip and the car is in the barriers, its race over.

The idea for the race came from Anthony Noghes, president of the Monegasque car club and close friend of the ruling Grimaldi family. The town was already host to the Monte Carlo rally, but Noghes conceived cars racing wheel-to-wheel through the streets. Even in the 1920s, the course was considered very narrow for such an event, but the inaugural race of 1929 – won by William Grover-Williams in a Bugatti – was considered a big success in attracting custom and prestige to

the area, and it has continued, on and off, to this day. It is the venue of choice for team sponsors to attend.

The course traces its way up a hill cut out of the cliff face and via the blind exit of Massenet corner into Casino Square. There, with the Casino on one side and the Hôtel de Paris on the other, the cars weave their way to the top of the hill that leads them down to Mirabeau, a very tight right-hander leading on to an even tighter left-hander, Loews. Taken in first gear at no more than 48km/h (30mph), this is the slowest corner in Grand Prix racing. Drivers have to be very careful to allow themselves enough room to get round, and cars frequently have extra steering lock made available to prevent the embarrassment of not being able to manage it. After a couple of successively quicker right-handers, the cars enter the famous tunnel, cut through solid rock beneath the Hôtel de Paris. After a flat-out kink in the middle, the cars exit the dim light at around 290km/h (180mph) before extreme braking for a first-gear chicane. The track then follows the harbour

◄ **The start of the race: eventual winner Michael Schumacher (Ferrari) leads the field towards Massenet in 2001.**

▼ **Chris Amon (Ferrari 312), in third, passes the fatal accident of Lorenzo Bandini at the 1967 Monaco Grand Prix.**

▲ **Ayrton Senna (McLaren) fends off Nigel Mansell's Williams during the closing stages to win at Monaco in 1992. Mansell had earlier been forced to pit while leading.**

Tabac

Piscine

Anthony Noghes

Saint Devote

Beau Rivage

Massenet

Casino

La Rascasse

Nouvelle Chicane

Mirabeau

Portier

Grand Hotel Hairpin

Loews Tunnel

Monte Carlo

Circuit length	3.370km (2.094 miles)
Lap record	1 min 14.545 secs K. Raikkonen 2003
Previous winners	2003 J. P. Montoya 2002 D. Coulthard 2001 M. Schumacher

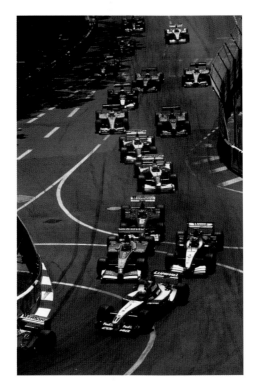

▲ Twenty-two cars are a tight squeeze through the streets of Monte Carlo on the first lap of the 2002 Monaco Grand Prix.

through Tabac, the swimming pool section and the slow Rascasse corner, before entering the pit straight on the way to Ste Devote, the right-hander that leads back up the hill to Casino.

Engineers will set the cars for Monaco with maximum wing settings, to give as much downforce as possible, as the low-speed nature of the track means there is very little penalty in drag. Suspensions will be set softer than usual, to allow for the bumps and to help traction out of the many slow, low-gear turns. The low-grip nature of the surface, and the lack of high-speed turns, means that tyre compounds are softer here than at any other track.

It is a circuit where drivers can make big gains by tuning into its rhythm, and there have been some notable Monaco specialists over the years, including five-time winners Graham Hill and Alain Prost. Ayrton Senna won the event six times between 1987 and 1993, while Michael Schumacher has met Prince Rainier on the top step of the podium five times since 1994.

▲ Michael Schumacher first took victory at Monaco in his Benetton B194 in 1994. He has since won it four times to date.

San Marino *Imola*

The principality of San Marino is used as a flag of convenience to give Italy two Grands Prix per season. The town of Imola is not in San Marino, but is around 145km (90 miles) south of Milan. The track is named in honour of Enzo Ferrari's son Dino, who worked for Ferrari but died from a illness in 1956, while still in his 20s.

The circuit was built in the 1960s, but it was not used for a Formula One Championship event until 1980, when it hosted the Italian Grand Prix, one of the few occasions that event was not held at Monza. Since 1981, the Italian Grand Prix has been back at Monza in its traditional September slot, while Imola takes an early-season space in the calendar.

One of only two anti-clockwise circuits in the schedule, it was originally a fast track, but has been constantly slowed by additional chicanes. This has made it one of the toughest circuits for brakes. The last round of changes came in the wake of the tragic events of 1994. Roland Ratzenberger was killed in qualifying when his Simtek left the track after damaging a front wing. The following day, Ayrton Senna died

◀ Nicola Larini, Michael Schumacher and Mika Häkkinen try not to show their emotions on the podium at Imola in 1994, following the tragic death of Ayrton Senna in the early laps of the race.

in the early laps of the race after his Williams left the track at the flat-out kink of Tamburello. After hitting the retaining wall at around 210km/h (130mph), a suspension component broke off and pierced his helmet.

Since then a chicane has been installed before Tamburello and a further one before "Villeneuve", the corner at which Ratzenberger lost his life. This corner was so named after Ferrari driver Gilles Villeneuve, who suffered a major accident here in 1980 as a result of a tyre blow-out.

It was at the 1989 San Marino Grand Prix that one of the biggest driver feuds in the sport's history was initiated.

Driving the dominant McLaren-Hondas, Ayrton Senna and Alain Prost had agreed between themselves that they would not fight out the first corner of the race, and that whichever of them got the better start would be given a clean passage by the other. For them, the race would effectively start after the first turn. It was Senna who made the better start and Prost duly tucked in behind for the first corner. They were in this order when, at the beginning of the fourth lap, Gerhard Berger suffered

▼ Finn Kimi Raikkonen's McLaren-Mercedes MP4/17 retired with exhaust problems after 44 laps at Imola in 2002.

Acque Minerale

Variante Alta

Piratella

Tosa

Villeneuve

Tamburello

Pit Lane

azza

ariante Bassa

Traguardo

4	201	8
4	154	
6	286	
3	123	14
	13	
15		
3	173	
6	290	16
2	94	
3	171	1
12	11	T2
9		
3	143	10
6	265	
6	289	
3	128	2
3		
4	249	4
T1		
5		
6	296	
4	222	6
2	109	7

Circuit Dino Ferrari

Circuit length	4.933km (3.065 miles)
Lap record	1 min 22.491 secs M. Schumacher 2003
Previous winners	2003 M. Schumacher 2002 M. Schumacher 2001 R. Schumacher

▶ Juan Pablo Montoya (Williams-BMW FW24) takes off at the Variante Alta during the San Marino Grand Prix at Imola in 2002.

an enormous accident in his Ferrari at Tamburello. The car hit the wall and burst into flames, and the race was stopped while he was released, amazingly with only light injuries.

The race was restarted, and this time Prost made the better start. He assumed Senna would not attack him into the first corner and did not drive defensively, but Senna chose to interpret their agreement as being valid only for the first start, and at the first corner he shot down the inside of his team-mate, and into the lead. He went on to win the race, with Prost a distant second. It was the sort of ruthlessness for which Senna was famous, but afterwards Prost was furious.

From that moment and until Prost's retirement at the end of 1993, the two greatest drivers of the era were at loggerheads with each other.

▶ Winner Nelson Piquet (Brabham BT49) at the Italian Grand Prix in 1980.

Spain *Barcelona*

The Barcelona circuit is known as the "laboratory of Formula One", owing to its extensive use as a test track by the teams in between races. It first hosted the Spanish Grand Prix in 1991, and since 1998 has held the event exclusively, though another Spanish track, at Jerez, hosted the European Grand Prix in 1997.

Built on industrial wasteland some miles north of the city, the circuit makes many conflicting demands of the cars. It has a long, long pit straight but this is immediately followed by a sequence of fairly tight second- and third-gear corners. Aerodynamic efficiency is therefore paramount here. The cars need fairly high wing settings to cope with the tighter corners, but those cars that can do this with the minimum penalty on drag for the long straight are the ones that do best.

◄ Graham Hill, 1969, and the high wing that caused his accident.

▼ David Coulthard gives his McLaren team-mate Mika Häkkinen a lift back after he had retired on the last lap while leading in 2001.

The advantage of an aerodynamically efficient car will always be exaggerated at this track. Long-duration turns and a coarse surface also mean it is very tough on tyres.

All these factors – and the season-long favourable weather – have helped give the circuit its testing popularity. If the car works well at Barcelona, it will tend to work well everywhere.

The 2001 race was a classic battle between two foes Mika Häkkinen and Michael Schumacher. The latter had led the early going in his Ferrari, with Häkkinen hanging on as best he could in second with the McLaren. Opting for longer stints between fuel stops than the Ferrari, Mika was hoping he would be able to gain the critical time needed after Michael made his stop. Schumacher made his first stop on lap 22, five short of Häkkinen's planned stop. Now leading, the Finn began pushing to the very limit in an attempt to build up the time needed to make his stop without losing position.

It wasn't quite enough, and after his stop Häkkinen rejoined just behind the Ferrari. Again though, he was fuelled for a longer stint, so giving him a second chance at pulling out the vital extra time after Schumacher made his second stop on lap 43. This time Häkkinen had seven laps on a low fuel load in which to build up the necessary cushion. Aided by Schumacher being slowed slightly by a vibration, Häkkinen this time was able to make his stop and exit just in front of the Ferrari. All he

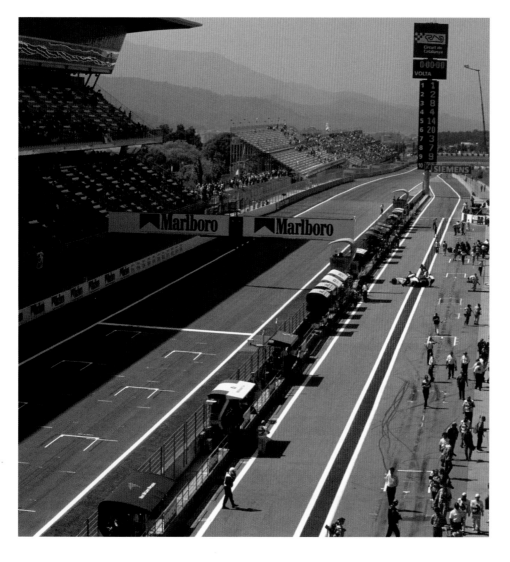

◄ The Barcelona start-finish straight and pit lane, with the Pyrennees mountains ever-present in the background.

Nissan

Campsa

Repsol

Banc Sabadell

New Holland

La Caixa

Renault

Elf

at

had to do now was stay there for the final 15 laps. It looked a relatively easy task for the Finn, who was notoriously cool under pressure.

The laps duly ticked away and, with Schumacher slowing even more, Häkkinen built up his lead to over half a minute. As he went past the pits for the last time, the McLaren's engine could be heard to be running rough. A few corners later, Mika pulled off to the side of the track. Michael couldn't believe his luck as he was handed victory on the last lap of the race.

On his slow-down lap, he stopped to give his disconsolate rival a lift back to the pits. Even Schumacher felt sorry for Häkkinen on that day.

▼ *(left)* Winner Mika Häkkinen (McLaren MP4-13) leads David Coulthard in the Spanish Grand Prix in 1998.

Circuit de Catalunya	
Circuit length	4.730km (2.939 miles)
Lap record	1 min 20.143 secs R. Barrichello 2003
Previous winners	2003 M. Schumacher 2002 M. Schumacher 2001 M. Schumacher

▼ Gerhard Berger leads McLaren team-mate Ayrton Senna into the first corner of the 1991 race. Winner Nigel Mansell is here in third, with Michael Schumacher fourth.

USA *Indianapolis*

F ormula One's biggest challenge in the modern era has always been how to open up the American market. Hosting a race in the world's biggest economy would naturally make the sport more attractive to sponsors and television companies looking for advertising revenue. Yet America has always had its own domestic race series, namely NASCAR stock cars and ChampCar single-seaters. Formula One meant little, if anything, to the average American television viewer.

There had been American Grands Prix at Watkins Glen in New York State through the 1960s and 1970s, but in the end they became economically unviable. In the 1970s and 1980s, Formula One dallied with street circuits in Long Beach, Detroit, Phoenix and Las Vegas. But part of the problem was the slow average speeds to which the cars were limited. To race fans brought up on a diet of lap speeds in excess of 320km/h (200mph) from both NASCAR saloons and ChampCar single-seaters on their super-fast oval tracks, Formula One hardly captured the imagination.

Using Indianapolis as a venue for a new American Grand Prix from 2000 was an inspired idea. Virtually every

American knew about Indianapolis, home of "the world's greatest race", the Indy 500. This ChampCar race had run since 1911 and was part of the very fabric of American life, one of the great sporting classics. By holding a Formula One race here, Grand Prix racing would benefit from the fame of the venue.

However, the famous banked speed bowl was not a suitable circuit for a Formula One machine. Instead, a new circuit was constructed that used part of the traditional track, but which then veered off into an infield of more or

▲ Michael Schumacher spins his Ferrari F1-2000, but still goes on to win the USA Grand Prix at Indianapolis in 2000.

▼ *(left)* Juan Pablo Montoya's Williams-BMW FW23 leads the field around the famous Indy banking in 2001.

▼ *(right)* Mika Häkkinen celebrates what would turn out to be his final Grand Prix victory before retirement in 2001. He is flanked by Michael Schumacher *(left)* and McLaren team-mate David Coulthard.

Indianapolis	
Circuit length	4.192km (2.605 miles)
Lap record	1 min 11.473 secs M. Schumacher 2003
Previous winners	2003 M. Schumacher 2002 R. Barrichello 2001 M. Häkkinen

less conventional Formula One track configuration. After 12 corners this rejoined the existing track on the banking of what is "Turn One" in ChampCar parlance, but which became Turn 13 of the Formula One track, given that the cars were travelling clockwise, the opposite way to the Champcars.

The Formula One circuit covered only a fraction of the area of the speedway, leaving the huge grandstands of three-quarters of the oval deserted. Yet even this made for over 200,000 spectators, well up on most European venues. Since 2000, the event has begun the slow task of turning America on to Formula One.

▼ Jarno Trulli (*left*) and Jenson Button about to clash in the early laps of the USA Grand Prix at Indianapolis. This was their second tangle in three races. The pair later became team-mates at Renault.

Index

PICTURE CREDITS
All photographs supplied by
Sutton Motorsport Images
except for the following.
t = top; b = bottom; l = left;
r = right; c = centre
Malcolm Jeal 20br; 28bl; 50t, tr, b.
Ludvigsen Library 21cl, b; 23tl, tr; 28t; 29t, c; 40t, c, br; 49t, b; 52; 55b; 68b; 72c; 74t, bl, br; 83b; 86t; 88t, b, c; 93b; 95t; 96t, c, b; 104t; 107t, b; 109br; 112b.
National Motor Museum 92t, b; 95b; 98t, b; 101t, c; 18t, bl, br; 21t; 29b; 49c; 59t, c, b; 72t, b; 79t, b.